Aligning
Student Support
With
Achievement
Goals

Aligning
Student Support
With
Achievement
Goals

THE SECONDARY PRINCIPAL'S GUIDE

Karen Seashore Louis
Molly F. Gordon

CORWIN PRESS
A SAGE Publications Company
Thousand Oaks, California

For information:

Corwin Press
A Sage Publications Company
2455 Teller Road
Thousand Oaks, California 91320
www.corwinpress.com

Sage Publications Ltd.
1 Oliver's Yard
55 City Road
London EC1Y 1SP
United Kingdom

Sage Publications India Pvt. Ltd.
B-42, Panchsheel Enclave
Post Box 4109
New Delhi 110 017 India

Printed in the United States of America

Library of Congress Cataloging-in-Publication Data

Louis, Karen Seashore.
Aligning student support with achievement goals: The secondary principal's guide / Karen Seashore Louis, Molly F. Gordon.
        p. cm.
Includes bibliographical references and index.
ISBN 1-4129-1659-3 (cloth) — ISBN 1-4129-1660-7 (pbk.)
    1. Student assistance programs—United States. 2. Counseling in secondary education—United States. I. Gordon, Molly F. II. Title.
LB3430.5.L68 2006
373.14—dc22   2005019607

This book is printed on acid-free paper.

05   06   07   08   09   10   9   8   7   6   5   4   3   2   1

Acquisitions Editor:	Elizabeth Brenkus
Editorial Assistants:	Candice L. Ling and Desirée Enayati
Production Editor:	Laureen A. Shea
Copy Editor:	Stacey Shimizu
Typesetter:	C&M Digitals (P) Ltd.
Proofreader:	Annette Pagliaro
Indexer:	Naomi Linzer
Cover Designer:	Rose Storey

Contents

Acknowledgments

This book emerges from a multiyear project that involved many people and organizations whose contributions need to be acknowledged. The Transforming School Counseling Initiative (TSCI) was a national endeavor sponsored and funded by the Wallace–Reader's Digest Fund, now reorganized as the Wallace Foundation. The project's immediate purpose was to improve school counseling in public schools by transforming the graduate-level preparation of counselors. The overarching goal, however, was to help students succeed academically—especially students living in low-income communities and students of color.

As part of this program, six universities were funded to carry out the work of transformation. The Education Trust, a nonprofit organization, provided both the initial framework for the effort and a source of support for all participants. Without the participation of the staff and students at these institutions, and in the districts with which they cooperated, this book would not have been possible. We particularly want to thank the principal investigators and faculty at those sites who have been our colleagues, coresearchers, and constant critical friends over the past five years. They are the following:

The Education Trust: Pat Martin and Reese House

California State University, Northridge: Charlie Hansen and Tovah Sands

Indiana State University, Terre Haute: Peggy Hines

The Ohio State University, Columbus: Susan Sears

State University of West Georgia: Brent Snow and Paul Phillips

University of Georgia, Athens: Richard Hayes and Pam Paisley

University of North Florida, Jacksonville: Carolyn Stone

At the University of Minnesota, many colleagues and graduate students participated in the project. We want to acknowledge particularly Lisa Jones, Pat Seppanen, John Romano, and Heidi Barajas, whose insights about student support and change in schools deeply influenced what we have written. We want especially to acknowledge Dan LaBore and Carol Freeman for their insight into the everyday lives of school support staff, teachers, administrators, and students. Without Dan Bratton's decisive editorial assistance, our sentences would be less precise and more jargon filled.

At the Wallace–Reader's Digest Fund/Wallace Funds, our initial project officer, Ian Beckford, asked for (and we hope received) intellectual rigor and commitment to the research goals of our grant. Ed Pauly, Director of Evaluation, championed our work during the last two years.

Finally, we want to thank all of the guidance counselors and principals who generously donated their time to discuss their own school experiences and to share their unique stories for this project. Throughout this book, we have used their words and experiences to illustrate our points. Although in many cases we are reporting on exceptional work, we have chosen to use pseudonyms for all of our examples.

—Karen Seashore Louis
—Molly F. Gordon
Minneapolis, Minnesota

Publisher's Acknowledgments

Mary Lynne Derrington, Superintendent
Blaine School District
Blaine, WA

Kathy Grover, Director of Curriculum
Clever Public Schools
Clever, MO

Stephen Handley, Principal
Terry High School
Terry, MS

Susan Hodges, Supervisor, Leadership Academy
Missouri Department of Elementary and Secondary Education
Jefferson City, MO

Paul Katnik, Supervisor, Leadership Academy
Missouri Department of Elementary and Secondary Education
Jefferson City, MO

Dan LaBore, Bush Program Project Coordinator
Saint Paul Public Schools
Saint Paul, MN

Joseph Murphy, Professor of Education
Peabody College
Vanderbilt University
Nashville, TN

Carolyn Stone, Associate Professor, President Elect, American School
    Counselor Association
University of North Florida
Jacksonville, FL

Janice Tkaczyk, Guidance Director, North Atlantic
    Vice President, American School Counselor Association
Cape Cod Technical High School
Harwich, MA

About the Authors

 **Karen Seashore Louis** is professor of Educational Policy and Administration at the University of Minnesota–Twin Cities. A past president of Division A of the American Educational Research Association (AERA), she is a widely published author in the field. Her recent books (all of which except for the last are co-authored) include *Organizational Learning in Schools* (1998); *Handbook of Educational Administration,* 2nd edition (1999); *Leadership for Change and School Improvement: International Perspectives* (2000); and *Organizing for School Change* (2005).

 **Molly F. Gordon** is a Research Fellow at the Center for Applied Research and Educational Improvement at the University of Minnesota. She received her MA in Educational Policy Studies from the University of Wisconsin–Madison, and is currently a PhD student in Educational Policy at the University of Minnesota–Twin Cities. Her recent research has focused on issues of leadership in school reform.

Before We Begin . . .

Please complete the quiz below to help focus on where you are and where you want to go.					
For each statement, circle the number that best reflects the situation in your school.	True	Somewhat True	Somewhat False	False	Don't Know
(1) Student support staff have detailed written job descriptions.	5	4	3	2	1
(2) I always know what my student support staff members are doing on a day-to-day basis.	5	4	3	2	1
(3) My student support staff seldom perform administrative duties, such as test administration.	5	4	3	2	1
(4) Most teachers understand the role of counselors or other student support staff.	5	4	3	2	1
(5) Student support staff are *not* responsible for handling most parent complaints or concerns.	5	4	3	2	1
(6) Counselors are *not* assigned students by last name or grade.	5	4	3	2	1
(7) Student support staff are part of the administrative team.	5	4	3	2	1
(8) Student support staff are actively involved in our efforts to improve student achievement.	5	4	3	2	1
(9) Teachers and student support staff work together to solve issues related to student achievement.	5	4	3	2	1
(10) Student support staff have annual professional development objectives.	5	4	3	2	1

(Continued)

(Continued)

Add all the numbers that you have marked:

- If your score is more than 45, your student support programs are probably functioning reasonably well, although you may want to look at this book for additional ideas to fine-tune your program. Chapters 2 and 4 may be most useful.
- If your score is between 30 and 44, your student development programs definitely need to be renewed. This book will be a useful guide.
- A score of less than 30 indicates significant untapped potential for creating sustained improvement in student achievement in your school.

*This book is dedicated to Dan Bratton, who provides Karen
Seashore Louis with both unswerving support and honest criticism,
and to Stephanie Johnson, who provides Molly Gordon
with endless encouragement and strength.*

The Gaping Hole in School Reform 1

In this chapter you will

- Learn that you cannot reach your student achievement goals without rethinking your school's use of human resources.
- Look at the role of student support personnel as part of your school's reform solution.
- Review some basic assumptions about how to make change happen in your school.
- See an overview of the rest of the book and what the book can do for you.

Student support personnel—the counselors, social workers, nurses, and other professionals who work in the school, but generally not in the classroom—have been little affected by the reform movements sweeping the American educational system in recent decades. This is because their efforts are viewed as tangential to student achievement and their contributions too diffuse and indirect to measure. Their job descriptions have evolved in isolation from the main structures of the school without any centralized or rigorous assessment of their efficiency or effectiveness. Our book is an effort to help you, the principal, design your own program to integrate the student support personnel with your school's overall achievement goals.

THE CASE FOR REFORM

The National Association for Secondary School Principals' (NASSP) influential report on high schools, *Breaking Ranks II*, outlines three principles for reform:[1]

1. Change the school's culture through collaborative leadership, professional learning communities, and the strategic use of data

2. Personalize the school environment

3. Increase the rigor and quality of curriculum, instruction, and assessment

The visionary agenda outlined in this report uses a strong research base to support these three themes. We agree with the directions suggested, and with the recommendations for action, but we also notice a gap that *Breaking Ranks II*, like the reform proposals that came before it, overlooks. All reform initiatives acknowledge that the main instruments for change are the professionals, students, and communities that are stakeholders of the schools. The emphasis on professionals, however, is given almost exclusively to teachers and administrators. School leaders have consistently overlooked the central role that student support personnel can play in achieving the three central goals outlined in *Breaking Ranks II*.

We know that student learning is directly affected by teachers. We also know that schools are steered by the decisions and daily work of school and district administrators. Nevertheless, an exclusive focus on administrators and teachers in school reform ignores critical resources that lie fallow in most schools.

This book argues that school administrators have resources at hand that are rarely well harnessed to school improvement goals: the professional staff members that are usually designated under the label of *student support*—specifically the counselors, social workers, home-school coordinators, and other professional groups sited in the school that are considered peripheral to the primary task of teaching.[2] Some schools—schools that we will highlight later on—have already enlarged the leadership tent to include student support staff members as core members of school improvement teams, but most schools have followed the reform movement's implicit assumption that improvements in learning will be led by teachers. Every educator who attends a district professional development workshop or a state association meeting is familiar with the call to engage teacher leadership, but how many have attended sessions that emphasize a more productive use of their counseling staff? This common oversight leaves administrators playing with less than a full deck.

THE FOCUS OF EDUCATIONAL REFORM LEGISLATION

The stark and consistent report of decline in U.S. education is empirically debatable.[3] What is evident is that the perception of serious problems has generated successive reform efforts that wash through American schools with increasing force. For the last two decades, school reform has been driven by a well-documented gap in student learning that exists between U.S. secondary schools and those in other countries, and the divide in achievement between minority and low-income children and their more advantaged peers.[4] U.S. elementary school students perform relatively well in some international studies, such as the Third International Math and Science Study, but decline begins with and accelerates during the adolescent years. The variability in student achievement between schools is just as worrying, in part because it is greater than in most other developed countries.[5]

An increasing number of education reform programs have been offered to (and often imposed on) U.S. secondary schools in the last two decades. Major restructuring efforts have centered on standards and accountability reforms: deregulation, changes in collective bargaining, school finance reforms, restructuring district offices, decentralized decision-making, and nationalized educational goals. When radical tinkering with existing schools disappoints, alternative models of delivering education are proposed, including school choice, vouchers, private contracting, and home-school networks. School principals are regarded as the fulcrum that levers these theories into action at the classroom level, but the reports and recommendations have not, with the exception of *Breaking Ranks II*, provided useable guides for action.[6] The best attempts to design comprehensive schoolwide reform models, which were highly touted during the late 1990s, appear to be less successful in high schools than in elementary schools,[7] perhaps in part due to the size and complexity of schools at the secondary level.[8] Most secondary schools have found comprehensive schoolwide reform a daunting task, and are using either process-based models that allow for a great deal of local development and adaptation (such as the Coalition of Essential Schools) or have moved to deal first with the problem of size by creating schools within schools.

Whatever initiatives or models are chosen locally, state policymakers have increasingly taken the lead as architects of a coherent and systematized educational program—one that includes high content standards and accompanying accountability measures. Policies of *curriculum upgrading*, as some call them, have been the states' response to calls for reform.[9] These mandates from the state level include increasing course requirements in academic subjects, developing curriculum frameworks and standards, initiating various types of student assessment, and providing staff development. Research suggests that the effectiveness of these policies at the state level is improved when there is coherence among them.[10] Legislating this coherence comes at a cost, however, as school administrators are shoehorned into a narrow, one-size-fits-all box.

The Secondary School Principal's Job

The following extract speaks to the role of the principal in a secondary school:

Traditional responsibilities of principals such as ensuring a safe environment, managing the budget, and maintaining discipline are still in force. . . . However, higher expectations for student success have often brought with them increased programming. In successfully implementing new programs, principals hire and supervise more people, enforce new policies, create new procedures, and provide support for the programs and all the associated auxiliary activities. Although programming has been expanding, responsibilities in other areas have not been reduced. In many cases, the additional resources principals need to provide leadership and support have not been forthcoming.

Other non-instructional responsibilities, such as greater professional accountability and increased expectations regarding home-school communication . . . have contributed to the complexity of the principalship. Concurrently, as considerable decision making has been decentralized to local schools, few clear guidelines are provided concerning which responsibilities will be the principals' and which will remain at the district level. . . . All of these dynamics make the management component of the principal's role ever more difficult.[12]

WHAT DO WE KNOW ABOUT INCREASING STUDENT ACHIEVEMENT?

School improvement, while difficult, is not a mystery. Several decades of sustained research in many countries point to a robust set of findings about what matters most if we want to increase student learning. We will not review that research here because good, practical summaries are available on a regular basis through magazines such as *Phi Delta Kappan* and *Educational Leadership*. But two points are worth making.

First, Teachers and Curriculum Count Most

The school reform conversation is correct in its assumption that what happens in the classroom—the immediate teaching and learning environment—is the best predictor of whether or not students will succeed in school. The Education Trust, a strong proponent of school reform, often contrasts the most popular explanation for variable achievement (students' family circumstances) with findings suggesting that teacher quality and a rigorous curriculum can make a greater difference.[13] This finding corresponds to the experience of parents who know that their children blossomed under some teachers while wilting under others.

Second, Teachers Don't Work Alone

Multiple studies suggest that the quality of school administrators also has an impact on student achievement, accounting for as much as 25% of the differences between schools.[14] In addition, many of the factors that explain differences between schools, such as school mission, leadership style, and the relationship with parents and the wider community, are also factors over which the principal has considerable influence. While principals may occasionally feel powerless to change the lives of their students because they have limited direct contact with them, their behavior and skill in structuring and guiding the actions of others is critical.

Which brings us back to the focus of this book: emerging research demonstrates that student support personnel can also have a significant impact on student learning, over and above that contributed by individual teachers. If this is the case, why are the reform reports so silent on the topic of student support professionals?

STUDENT SUPPORT PERSONNEL: A 10% SOLUTION?

How many principals wouldn't jump at the chance to add more person power to their school reform initiatives? In a recent study, two-thirds of the principals surveyed indicated that they simply did not have the personnel necessary to raise student achievement to mandated levels.[15] One often advocated solution is to increase productivity by making better use of the resources that are already in the school.[16] While this may feel a bit like changing the tires on a moving bus, it is realistic to assume that federal, state, and local governments will not be rushing to meet the requests for additional funding that most districts continue to make. Under these conditions, if improvement occurs at the school level, it will be through continuous improvement, which necessitates resource reallocation.[17] In our view, based on three years of research conducted in seven metropolitan school districts, one of the most underutilized groups in many schools is the group of student support professionals already on-site.

It is difficult to determine how many professionals are employed in student support programs in most secondary schools, in part because the field is not well defined. One recent national report on student guidance limits its investigation to school guidance counselors.[18] In some schools, guidance counseling is in a separate organizational unit from other personnel who serve student needs (e.g., social workers, home-school coordinators, etc.), while in other schools they are housed together. Counselors perform functions in some schools that are assigned to social workers in others—and vice versa. In other words, there is no common organizational design for student support services, but rather an ad hoc evolution of roles within each school.

Based on the information that is available, however, it seems that in a typical secondary school in the mid-1990s approximately 6% of the budget went to counselors and school psychologists.[19] This figure is, of course, an underestimate of the total student support programs budget in many schools, where today you might also find a home-school coordinator, a chemical dependency professional, social workers, and others with related training. We have reviewed the Web sites of junior high/middle schools and high schools located in the states that were part of our study, and conclude that between 10% and 20% of the professional staff in any school are neither administrators nor teachers. Of these, most are involved in student support programs of various kinds. This is congruent with older data currently available from the National Center for Educational Statistics. Thus, approximately 10% of each school's professional staff is disconnected from the school's major mission and goals. These figures lead us to label efforts to integrate student support personnel in school improvement goals *the 10% solution* (even though in your school it might be the 14% or even the 19% solution). In short, use your resources better!

Throughout this book, we will consider ideas and approaches that are applicable to all student support professionals. We freely acknowledge, however, that school or guidance counselors dominate the field of student support because of their sheer numbers, the research involving their roles, and the initiatives designed to improve their effectiveness. In this way, much of the data and research presented in this book evolved from our work specifically with school counselors. Where possible, we have expanded our discussion to involve other student support professionals, such as social workers. Throughout this book, we ask you to keep in mind that all professionals ministering to specific needs in your student population can have a place in your school that harmonizes their efforts with overall achievement goals.

As we interviewed principals in our study, we were surprised at how many of them knew little about what their student support personnel did—other than the most visible tasks of scheduling and handling persistent social problems. As we shall see later in this book, student support personnel are often dissatisfied with the way in which their time is spent and perceive themselves as marginalized within their schools. This suggests an opportunity for a school-by-school resource analysis.

Of course, another solution to the problem that the work of many professional staff is not directed toward core school goals would be to reallocate money currently dedicated to student support elsewhere. Some new schools and charter schools have chosen to eliminate specialized student support positions entirely, devoting the additional resources to more teachers and smaller classroom size. Even in "regular" schools that have not made such a strategic decision, there is some evidence that the current round of budget cuts may have fallen disproportionately on student support staff.[20] As more and more schools implement site-based management, principals are deciding staffing needs and programming, and they are often empowered to determine, for example, whether a technology coordinator or a counselor makes more sense for the school. These are difficult decisions when allowed, but approximately 25 states mandate counselors in secondary schools while others require social workers to support special education programs. State policy thus narrows a school leader's options.

This book will neither address all staffing options nor advocate for one solution over another. We will, however, explore such questions as the following:

- *Are counselors and other support staff well-used resources in the effort to increase student learning?* This is the focus of Chapter 2, where we look at emerging models that link student support programs and academic achievement.
- *What structural features of the typical secondary school interfere with the work of student support staff?* Chapter 3 goes into this in more detail, using data from our study of the role of school counselors.
- *What is a principal's "mental model" of the role and value of student support, and how does this mental image help or hinder counselors' efforts to focus on improving student achievement?* Chapter 4 uses case studies of schools to illustrate the impact that principals have had on new roles for student support staff.
- *What can principals do to implement the 10% solution?* Drawing on our own data, and on the broad array of research about leadership in and out of schools, we provide a number of practical suggestions in Chapters 5 and 6.

Before we move into the core of the book, we need to make clear some of the foundations that provide a basis for our analysis and recommendations. Although we are researchers, we have worked extensively on the topic of change in schools and have often engaged in collaborative co-construction of ideas with principals and other school professionals. We also believe that it is important to base our recommendations to principals on what we know from decades of research about leadership for change. We make one unequivocal assumption: Principals are not just one agent of change in a school environment—they are *the* change masters. They are the eye of the needle that outside forces must pass through. Their understanding and direction sets the tone and provides the motivation for structural and cultural changes within a school.

THE PRINCIPAL AS CHANGE MASTER

Change masters are—literally—the right people in the right place at the right time. The right people are the ones with the ideas that move beyond the organization's established practice, ideas they can form into visions. The right places are the integrative environments that support innovation, encourage the building of coalitions and teams to support and implement visions. The right times are those

> *moments in the flow of organizational history when it is possible to reconstruct reality on the basis of accumulated innovations to shape a more productive and successful future.*
>
> —Rosabeth Moss Kanter

The term *change master* was coined by Harvard Business School professor Rosabeth Moss Kanter in the early 1980s to highlight the "new" role of top business executives.[21] The concept of change master quickly caught on, and a trickle of early books on managing change has today become a torrent. A short list of our favorites is included in the Resources section at the end of this chapter.

A few key change management principles translate easily to the approach that we take in this book. We present them here, with limited discussion, to ensure that we are on the same page. We will return to them in Chapter 5, with specific guidance for how to renew the student support system in your school.

Removing Barriers

Improving schools is inherently difficult, chaotic, and unpredictable. The most intractable problems that schools face are rooted in multiple systems that have histories and connections to other systems. A student's behavior and performance is deeply affected by invisible forces that exist outside the school and the school's formal culture. Problems such as these are referred to as "wicked," because the proposed solution cannot address the whole cause, may reveal or exacerbate other issues, or cannot be implemented due to flaws within the solution itself. The issues faced by schools that are asked to do more with less are "wicked" instead of "tame." [22] This means that they are not amenable to solutions through traditional linear change processes and management-initiated activities, which include most forms of the diagnosis–planning–implementation–evaluation chain.

Much of the change literature (including most of the books that we recommend) focuses on the challenge of transformational leadership for change—an individual or some group that has a vision for a new way of doing things and is able to persuade others to follow them. In reality, under most circumstances, getting people to change requires more than vision, charisma, and persistence. Over the years, we have studied educators attempting to implement change and have observed that many begin with the idea that they only need to augment what they are already doing well. Schools accumulate new programs, new resources, professional development, and even new staff members, and the results never quite meet expectations. Anthony Bryk and his colleagues observed, based on studying the massive Chicago school reforms of the last decade, that schools can be like Christmas trees: They collect new resources and add baubles, but the new ornaments don't change the nature of the tree.[23]

Kurt Lewin, one of the founders of modern psychology and action research, concluded that change requires understanding both the positive features of the group that press toward change and the (often hidden) barriers that press with equal force to maintain the status quo. Steering an organization by only adding pressure to change rarely works: Successful change requires recognizing the barriers, and removing those that can be addressed. Only when the equilibrium is altered can real change occur.

More than 25 years ago, Seymour Sarason pointed out that schools have so many deeply embedded features that merely reinforcing the positive will not result in real change.[24] Even when everyone agrees that change is desirable, change does not always occur. Some barriers must be accepted or viewed as problems requiring long-term solutions. Resistant teachers can grow deep roots, and schools must take as a given the socioeconomic circumstances of their students. The task of the educational change master is to navigate around the immobile barriers while identifying and spotlighting impediments that have solutions.

Preconditions for Change

Change does not occur in schools until knowledge, along with an image of the desired change, is translated into action. The change master in any school must tackle five preconditions in order to accomplish any real change:[25]

1. **Clarity.** The ideas for improvement must be understood clearly; they cannot be fuzzy, vague, or confusing.

2. **Relevance.** The changes in people's roles must be seen as meaningful, as connected to their normal professional life and concerns.

3. **Action Images.** The principles underlying the proposed changes must be exemplified in specific actions, clearly visualized. People must have an image of "what to do to get there."

4. **Will.** There must be motivation, interest, and action orientation— a will to *do* something.

5. **Skill.** People must be capable of doing what is envisioned. Without skill, the changes will be abandoned or so distorted as to be unrecognizable.

We have labeled these as preconditions, but that does not mean that they must all be lined up together on the starting line. On the contrary, although it is difficult to initiate change without some attention to each of these five issues, their real meaning will emerge as school staff members grapple with the significance of change in their lives. As Gene Hall and Shirley Hord pointed out several decades ago, each stage in the change process, from the first meeting to discuss whether change is needed to the reviews of evaluation data years later, requires individuals to adjust and reinterpret what they know.[26] One of the responsibilities of the change master is to choreograph this interpretive process.[27]

Anticipating and Adjusting: The Performance Dip Phenomenon

The change master must be aware of the stages of change and antici-pate the emotions that usually accompany them. Unless the orchestrators of the process anticipate what will happen, they cannot easily predict where to place their energies or where to encourage other people to place theirs. We find particularly useful the idea of the *performance dip* (some-times referred to as the *implementation dip*), described by several authors. *Performance dip* refers to the fact that most changes, even those which ultimately prove beneficial, will initially interrupt the smooth functioning of the way things were and will therefore appear counterproductive in the short run.

Figure 1.1 illustrates the stages of change, the associated emotions, and the actions on the part of the change master that are required to keep the school on course.[28] The figure shows three stages of change: ini-tiation, implementation, and institutionalization (or routinization). The arrows at the top of the figure denote some of the work that needs to be done by all members of the school if they are to move toward real, sus-tainable change. These are the practical steps that must be taken to deal with the issues of clarity, relevance, action images, will, and skill. The arrows at the bottom of the figure suggest some of the actions that are the responsibility of the change masters, and they incorporate the obser-vation by Michael Huberman and Matthew Miles that providing both pressure and support for change are the personal responsibility of school leaders.[29]

If you are not familiar with the basic principles of change manage-ment portrayed in Figure 1.1, you should turn to the Resource list at the end of this chapter before making major shifts in redefining the roles of teachers and counselors in your school. If you see yourself as a novice, we strongly recommend the books by Michael Fullan, Gene Hall and Shirley Hord, and John Kotter.[30] If you consider yourself an experienced change master, but want to freshen up your knowledge, the other books on the list will deepen your perspectives.

Before we leave this overview, however, there is a third topic that is not well covered by the books in the resource list, but which is particularly important for redefining professional roles in schools.

Figure 1.1   Performance Dip Model

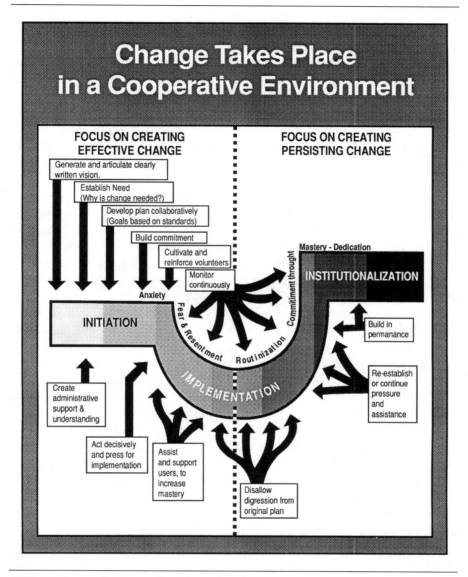

SOURCE: Eastwood & Louis (1992). Used with permission of Scarecrow Education, an imprint of Rowan & Littlefield Publishing Group.

Enter Distributed Leadership

The concept of *distributed leadership* is currently popular in the educational literature. The assumption is simple: If you have too much to do, and all of it is important, you have to decide to give some jobs and decisions away. Rather than simply delegating individual decisions and short-term jobs, distributed leadership makes sharing of responsibilities a permanent change in the way business gets done inside the school. Distributed leadership is essential when change involves redefining what people do and with whom they work. Both researchers and practitioners have come to advocate this management philosophy as a partial solution to the ever-expanding responsibilities of principals.

This decentralization of responsibility is occurring at the same time that states and the federal government are engaging in efforts to legislate learning. All educational professionals, not just principals, are increasingly told to make changes in their work lives: to make more professional decisions about their work, to expand their notion of professionalism, and to decentralize authority from remote locations to local sites of practice. Devolution of authority brings with it greater responsibility at the school site and for the change master.

The teacher leadership literature emphasizes leadership roles exercised by those who are not in formal positions of authority.[31] In contrast to this view, distributed-leadership research starts with the inclusion of teacher leaders as more formal decision makers. This contrast is not a mere nuance of perspective, but reflects a change in the way more schools are being organized. Rather than thinking about the school as clearly defined zones of influence, in which administrators make policy and resource allocation decisions while teachers decide what and how to teach, Mark Smylie and his colleagues point out that distributed leadership stresses the importance of shifting our "attention away from individual and role-based conceptions of leadership and toward organizational and task-oriented conceptions of leadership."[32]

This blending of teacher empowerment with traditional principal leadership functions has not yet enveloped the broader set of professionals in the school. The multidirectional and fluid nature of social influence can affect the performance of a school in different ways, and if important groups, such as student support personnel, are not part of the networks of influence and decision making, solidarity around school improvement goals and strategies becomes more difficult to achieve. The complex decisions involved in working with students demand collaborative and integrative roles and a shared commitment to the common goals.

The issue of how to achieve this in the context of increasing pressures and in the midst of internal and external conflict is constantly on the minds of principals. And, as Peter Gronn points out, the best way of tracking distribution of responsibilities is not to look at rhetoric, but at how labor is actually divided and how leadership teams are constructed.[33] We have observed in our work that it is still unusual to find a student support professional on a school leadership team.

WHERE ARE WE GOING?

The emphasis of this book is on reorganizing the resources you already have as the best—and perhaps even the only—efficient way to get additional help without adding to the strain on your staff. We argue that in many secondary schools the most underutilized resources are found among the professionals who provide support to students inside the school but outside the classroom. In our book, we look at professionals who are currently working at the periphery of the school improvement agenda and outside of the direct attention of state accountability legislation. Better utilization of these highly trained school employees will help you to lever actions and opportunities that support the core focus on students and teachers. When teachers feel more supported, they are more willing to examine their role in the overall school improvement agenda.

This requires that you guide a change process that has some unusual characteristics. Student support services function in the margins of the school's main work and involve staff who may not now be working closely with each other or with teachers. School support personnel may not view themselves as being particularly connected to the student achievement agenda, a view that is reinforced by their having escaped accountability initiatives. Yet our research and the work of others suggests that the payoff from their integration into your school's improvement goals can be significant.

RESOURCES

A Dozen of Our Favorite
Popular Books on Change Management

The following books were selected because they contain durable ideas that will, especially if they are considered together, push almost anyone's ideas about change management beyond their current boundaries. In addition, they are all good reads and, although based in research, reflect an understanding of the problems of practice.

Bennis, W. (2000). *Managing the dream: Reflections on leadership and change.* Cambridge, MA: Perseus.

> Every leader needs to be familiar with Warren Bennis, a former university president as well as a decades-long advisor to CEOs. Bennis's contributions to understanding modern organizations are without parallel, and this book offers a collection of some of his previously published writing on change.

Fullan, M. (1993). *Change forces: Probing the depths of educational reform.* New York: Falmer.

> Michael Fullan is the foremost synthesizer of research on educational change. This book, which is the first (and we think still the best) of his series on change forces, outlines what we know about managing change in school settings. The second book, *Change forces: The sequel* (1999), and the third, *Change forces with a vengeance* (2003), elaborate on the ideas presented in this early book, and are also worth looking at. This book is, however, the most practical, and if you haven't read it, you should!

Hall, G., & Hord, S. (1987). *Change in schools: Facilitating the process.* Albany, NY: SUNY Press.

> The authors of this book provide a useful theory of how individual change occurs during an organizational change effort. Their first perspective, "Levels of Use,"

emphasizes the importance of gauging school-level change by understanding individual levels of familiarity and competence in taking on new behavior. The second perspective, "Stages of Concern," looks at the emotional aspects of change. The models have been developed as both research and monitoring tools over many years, and are used throughout the world.

Kotter, J. P. (1996). *Leading change.* Boston: Harvard Business School.

Kotter's book is one of the most popular among managers in the private sector. While not all business management texts are relevant to school administrators, this book provides an excellent overview of basic principles that we think are particularly relevant for principals. We particularly like Kotter's emphasis on how to provide a compelling vision for change and how to encourage people in the organization to come on board. Moreover, his discussion of how to generate short-term wins is an important antidote to long-term strategic plans that often weigh heavily on a tired change master.

Kouzes, J. M., & Posner, B. Z. (2002). *The leadership challenge.* San Francisco: Jossey-Bass.

This is a good companion book to Kotter's, because we consider both these books to be the best of the popular general management books that emphasize the role of leadership in change. Clearly, there are differences between business and school settings, but both of these books provide pointed summaries of what is known about strategic approaches to change. Kouzes and Posner use their deep experience to succinctly outline the challenges of leadership, summarizing the qualities that leaders must draw upon and the way in which these qualities need to be expressed in order to motivate and encourage others. Both this book and the work by Kotter focus on practices that can easily be adapted to educational settings.

Louis, K. S., & Miles, M. (1990). *Improving the urban high school: What works and why.* New York: Teachers College Press.

This is the only one of our recommended books that uses a lot of data—but it nevertheless develops a practical approach to managing the beginning stages of change when there are few resources, some hostile circumstances, and a sense of cynicism and fatigue among faculty members. While it is 15 years old, the case studies of five high schools are not particularly dated.

Mitroff, I. (1998). *Smart thinking for crazy times.* San Francisco: Berrett-Koehler.

Mitroff always thinks a little more "outside of the box" than most management writers. This book, although it might look like a management text, is really a primer on the critical questions that need to be asked as part of analyzing and changing an organizational system. A quick read, it focuses less on the leader and more on the complexity of problem solving. The first third of the book, which poses critical questions for analyzing system problems, is the best. Particularly important for school settings is the discussion of how to formulate problems and how to choose the right stakeholders.

Morgan, G. (1997). *Imaginization.* Thousand Oaks, CA: Sage.

Less a book than a collection of ideas and tools that you can use to help both yourself and those that you work with to see things differently, this work is invaluable. The materials speak to the heart and ideas that are often "beyond words" but help to shake up a meeting or a discussion so that people can move beyond current positions. Use it to challenge your own ideas or those of your school improvement team! And then go and read other books by Morgan.

Quinn, R. (1996). *Deep change.* San Francisco: Jossey-Bass.

Being a change manager means looking inward to the personal issues that are raised by change. This book presents some of the most critical ideas about personal change in the context of changing an organization and the lives of others. Without this book, you may inadvertently become part of the problem, in spite of your best efforts. What is the alternative to deep change on a personal level? Slow death. . . . Quinn argues persuasively that you cannot encourage others to make deep changes unless you are willing to make them yourself.

Sarason, S. (1996). *Revisiting the culture of the school and the problem of change.* New York: Teachers College Press.

This is a revision of Sarason's classic work on what needs to change in schools if student experiences and learning are to improve. Rather than looking at the quick fixes, Sarason concentrates on the basic features of school culture that make real change difficult. While this is not a quick read, it is essential for change masters who want to develop their own checklist of what needs to be altered in a school before significant change can occur. This is one of the few classic writings on change that pays a lot of attention to student experiences.

Schmoker, M. (1999). *Results: The key to continuous school improvement.* Arlington, VA: Association for Supervision and Curriculum Development.

This is the text for school leaders who want to understand what data-driven decision making can actually do for their schools. Schmoker provides practical examples of what needs to happen before the school can become a real learning organization. His focus on using data positively is a welcome antidote to the sense that data is largely used to punish schools, teachers, and students.

Weick, K., & Sutcliffe, K. (2001). *Managing the unexpected: Assuring high performance in an age of complexity.* San Francisco: Jossey-Bass.

Weick and Sutcliff's book is an invaluable tool for principals who are trying to create real change in classroom practices and student experiences while at the same time working effectively within a results-based accountability environment. The emphasis on continuous improvement is a refreshing alternative to change management books that emphasize only transformation and "big new thinking."

Old Versus New Models of Student Support Programs   **2**

In this chapter you will

- Review the history of student support programs in schools.
- Consider the old-model roles of student support staff.
- Get an overview of emerging "new model" reform initiatives in student support.
- Begin to diagnose the need for change in your school.

This chapter begins with an examination of how secondary schools have traditionally organized student support programs, focusing in particular on the evolution of the school counselor. We then move on to emerging models of student support programs, such as the Transforming School Counseling Initiative (TSCI), that have been developed by activists within the professions, including the American School Counselor Association (ASCA), and we will look at trends in other student support disciplines. Finally, we introduce an expanded comprehensive support program (CSP) that considers the multiprofessional nature of student support activities.

THE EMERGENCE OF STUDENT SUPPORT PROGRAMS IN THE 20TH CENTURY

Student support professionals became a feature in schools in the early 1900s in response to political, social, and economic events stemming from the industrial revolution and the influx of immigrants entering the workforce and schools.[1] School guidance was a response to the schools' expanding role in producing citizens in an increasingly technical and complex society. Initially, this role was provided as a volunteer service by middle-class women, until the need for more systematic school-based services demanded regular, full-time employees. This was often the truant officer, whose title implies a narrower role than counselors were soon expected to play.

Prior to the late 1800s, most students attended school only long enough to become literate, with high school graduation and college attendance limited to a few. The shift from a secondary school system that was focused on the elite to the so-called common school model, under which all students attended until they were 16 years old and were encouraged to stay until age 18, was profound.[2] To accommodate this new kind of student and provide the vocational education demanded by industry, schools added new curricula and career training to the school structure. The new role of guidance counselor developed as a mechanism to assist groups and individuals to consider these new types of careers in their own unfolding life patterns.[3] Consequently, counselor reforms became linked to broader vocational reforms in schools.

Equality and opportunity have been persistent American ideals, and schools quickly assumed a part in helping to give students the chance of a better life. This trend climaxed under President Lyndon Johnson's Great Society initiatives (variously known as *Title I* and *Chapter I*), which expanded the role of the school in mitigating barriers to students' achievement that were associated with poverty and race. In many cases, new funds were used to hire social workers, whose functions were primarily to link students in need with services outside of the school. By the 1970s, the number of social workers assigned to schools had grown so large that the National Association of Social Workers began a journal dedicated to this new subfield. By the 1990s, the focus of school social work had turned from "putting out fires" to the core notions of prevention and building resiliency.[4]

The once lonely school counselor has been joined more recently by additional staff members whose roles vary depending on school needs and funding opportunities. Many schools have specialized social workers who focus on the particular needs of special education students or other groups identified as being high-risk because of family poverty. Chemical dependency counselors, whose training is rather different from either social workers or traditional school counselors, are far more common now than just 20 years ago. The school nurse also has increasing responsibility for a broad range of health issues. Home-school coordinators don't usually have a professional degree to back up their work, but they have often replaced the attendance monitor as part of expanded efforts to strengthen school-family connections. Calls for increased community and parent involvement are coming from a variety of stakeholder groups.[5]

Dedicated school support professionals have increased in numbers and importance, but each role has evolved separately in response to specific issues. Few schools have a coherent plan for how support staff should work together to achieve the one goal that they all have in common: healthy, successful students. The resulting condition of modest disorganization was not addressed with the first major reform report of the 1980s, *A Nation at Risk*,[6] and has been, when mentioned at all, only a minor component of more recent efforts to develop comprehensive school reform models.[7] As a consequence, school counselors and their student support colleagues are treated as onlookers or even outsiders in the process of school change.

Even though the role of supporting students, whether through encouraging attendance or helping students to make choices, emerged from societal needs and pressures and has increased in complexity and size during the last 25 to 30 years, the function of student support professionals in the larger scheme of things has been largely ignored. The major texts used for training school administrators pay little attention to student support, and a recent search of Internet resources provides ample evidence that counselors and social workers are rarely linked to the significant agendas of school administration.

Our research suggests that student support programs are still dominated by school counselors, so we will begin our consideration of the role of student support staff with a look at this traditional role.

OLD MODEL OF STUDENT SUPPORT PROGRAMS

A Day in the Life of an Old-Model Counselor

Jenna, a high school counselor, arrives at work by 6:45 a.m. to get a jump on her mountains of paperwork. She has approximately 415 students and she needs to map out and input all of her students' course schedules for the next quarter into the computer. In the process, Jenna knows she must make careful decisions about the appropriate courses for each student—a mistake in one student's schedule can have lasting effects on the student's ability to graduate on time. Plus, Jenna doesn't want to go through what she did last year—processing a long line of students wishing to change their schedule because of glitches in the system.

By 8:30, Jenna has made some progress with the scheduling, but the rest of her morning is devoted to meeting with some of her students one-on-one. She can't help but remember what her principal said when she was first hired:

I want you to know everything you possibly can about your students, besides their grade history and where they're going to go to college. I want you to try to establish some type of personal rapport with each one, so that they can come to you with their needs, whether they are academic or personal.

Jenna feels overwhelmed by the sheer number of students, but the individual time she spends helping those who come to her with problems is the most satisfying part of her job.

During lunch hour, when Jenna is working hall duty, she hears a fight begin between groups of students. Jenna stops the fight, identifies the students, and tries to sort out the chain of events. The principal asks Jenna to meet individually with each student and then mediate with them as a group to prevent another flare up. The other counselors are inundated with their own work, so this unscheduled interruption takes up the rest of her afternoon—time she had planned to use to update her students' transcripts and begin documentation of duties for the career awareness day that is coming up. Instead, Jenna decides to work late, because she will be at the school early the next morning administering and proctoring the PSAT test and therefore will be unable to get back to scheduling until tomorrow afternoon.

The above case represents what we call the "old model" of student support. Jenna's day is largely consumed with paperwork; she only has time for a few students because she works one-on-one with them, yet she doesn't get as much done as she hopes because she is expected to handle the day-to-day crises of the school. Her principal expects her to get to know all of her students well—all 415! Her consultations with the school's social workers are episodic and usually involve "handing over" a student whose needs she cannot address.

As a principal, it is important for you to really look at the above case and ask yourself, "Is this the best use of Jenna's time?" How might you, as a principal, use Jenna in a more productive way?

This chapter will outline some of the old-model functions of school counselors and other student support professionals. Chapter 3 will go into more detail about these traditional functions and why we believe they are barriers to the 10% solution we alluded to in Chapter 1.

Traditional Student Support Roles

School counselors are not the only professionals frustrated by traditional role expectations in schools. In most districts there is no current written document outlining the role of social workers and no clear job description for other student support professionals. In other cases, the job expectations for social work professionals parallel Jenna's experience. For example, one vague social work job description that we encountered called for applicants to "perform other such social work functions related to the school program as appropriate," as well as to "perform other incidental tasks or services consistent with the job goal of this position." These are only two "essential functions" out of 32, ranging from monitoring student testing to evaluating the effectiveness of community services. (See the Resources section at the end of this chapter for the complete list.) This sweeping job description could leave any social worker wondering what his or her day-to-day work will actually entail. Even though funding structures might limit certain positions (such as a social worker or school psychologist hired under Title I to work with special education students), many principals are unaware of the flexibility they have in shaping the functions of student support staff to better align with student achievement.

The daily operation of schools encourages principals to use student support staff in multiple ways that do not necessarily carry out the mission statement. Each time a school gets a new principal, the jobs are informally renegotiated; the less experienced the principal, the less likely he or she is to be aware of how student support professionals might help students' academic achievement.[8] The following are examples of old-model student support roles that we have gathered from our research and that will be elaborated upon in Chapter 3:

- **Student Support Staff as "Gofers."** At an extreme, some student support personnel become "gofers" that facilitate other school functions between their responsibilities of managing unpredictable student crises. They are assigned tasks based on the perception that, because they do not teach classes, they have the flexibility to do multiple duties. A practical consequence of poorly defined roles is that the actual jobs of support personnel vary enormously, not only from district to district but even from school to school.
- **Student Support Staff as Paper Pushers and Testing Coordinators.** Paperwork is a never-ending task in all schools. The various administrative tasks assigned to student support staff members are related, loosely, to the academic goals. In some cases, scheduling of student classes is still done by hand—an important task for individual students, but one that could be performed by nonprofessional assistants using computer programs with assistance from the counselor. Paperwork has burgeoned with the expansion of state accountability legislation, which involves more monitoring of individual students and mountains of test results that must be handled carefully, as measuring student achievement has become a high-stakes activity. Student support staff members often wind up with this work because schools lack lower paid assistants or clerks to complete them.

- **Student Support Staff as Record Keepers.** Guidance counselors often complain that their time is consumed with scheduling and the manual review of student records. In some cases, a counselor is so inundated with paperwork (300–400 students per counselor is the usual minimum) that other professionals are hired for face-to-face interaction with students. Social workers face similar record-keeping expectations.

- **Student Support Staff as Disciplinarians.** Teachers and administrators in some schools view counselors and/or social workers as the school disciplinarians. This means that their day is filled with minor problems of student behavior, many of which should be addressed by improving teachers' classroom management skills.

- **Student Support Staff as Therapists.** Practicing school counselors and social workers received their preparation in university programs in which most, if not all, of their courses were focused on training family and individual therapists. The first substantive course in many programs is Introduction to Individual Counseling. This is, in fact, what many school counselors want to concentrate on—working with students individually or in small groups on mental health issues. Conversely, some mental health professionals argue that school counselors are not sufficiently trained in individual therapy to provide the appropriate services for the students most severely in need of them, and that their mental health services for the rest are largely "feel good" bandages.[9] In the same vein, many school-mandated social work tasks include working with children on an individual basis on social or emotional issues.[10] But as we will see later on in this chapter, working with students one-on-one is impractical for extremely large student caseloads.

EMERGING MODELS OF STUDENT SUPPORT PROGRAMS

The emerging new models for student support programs regard the above list of activities as distractions from the primary purpose of schools and school-based professionals. We agree with the newer models that the function of student support professionals in the school links more closely to increased student achievement. The school counseling profession, the largest provider of student support programs, has been the most vocal about this need for change. We believe their statements and principles apply equally well to their fellow student support professionals.

It is clear that expectations for schools have changed—all eyes are on student learning and preparation for future learning and success, not student mental health. The problem with the old-model indicators is that they are weakly associated with improved student learning and success beyond high school. In our studies, we have observed school support staff engaged in activities that *do* directly contribute to overall school achievement goals. In particular, we know from research that students who take more rigorous courses, who work harder and smarter in school, who have at least one adult who cares about them personally and supports their academic success, and who have access to the social services that permit them to attend school regularly will do better. These factors are the focus of the new-model student support program.

The limited research available on the correspondence between successful comprehensive guidance programs and academic success shows a positive effect on the social and mental health of students in addition to an increase in academic achievement. For example,

- "Students from more fully implemented guidance programs reported earning higher grades, being better prepared for the future, and having a more positive school environment than students from schools with less fully developed guidance programs."[11]
- "Students in more fully implemented guidance programs in Utah have higher college entrance examination scores, took more advanced classes, and rated their overall educational experience as better than students from less developed programs."[12]
- "Students in high implementation schools rated their overall educational preparation as more adequate; rated their job preparation as better; took more advanced mathematics and science courses; took more career and technical education courses; had higher ACT scores in every area of the test; and rated guidance and career planning services in their schools higher."[13]
- "School counseling interventions that focus on the development of cognitive, social and self-management skills can result in sizable gains in students' academic achievement."[14]
- "Strong scientific evidence demonstrates that increased student connection to school promotes educational motivation, classroom engagement and improved school attendance."[15]

Clearly, the role of a comprehensive student support program can be crucial in increasing academic achievement for all students. Therefore, we turn to emerging ideas and models that target student support to increasing student achievement. Again, because the school counseling profession has high visibility, we begin with the models that propose to transform the role of school counselors. Later in the chapter, we will argue that these models must be broadened into a comprehensive support program to include all student support professionals.

New-Model School Counseling Is . . .

According to the Education Trust, new-model counseling is

a profession that focuses on the relations and interactions between students and their school environment with the expressed purpose of reducing the effect of environmental and institutional barriers that impede student academic success.

The profession fosters conditions that ensure educational equity, access, and academic success for all students K–12. To accomplish this function, the trained school counselor must be an assertive advocate who creates opportunities for all students to nurture dreams of high aspirations. He or she assists students in their academic, social, emotional, and personal development, and help them to define the best pathways to successfully achieve their dreams.

Serving as leaders, as well as effective team members, school counselors work with teachers, administrators, and other school personnel to make sure that each student succeeds. As consultants, they can empower families to act on behalf of their children by helping parents/guardians identify student needs and shared interests, as well as access available resources.

The function necessarily requires focused attention to students for whom schools have been the least successful—poor students and students of color. A concentration is required on issues, strategies and interventions that will assist in closing the achievement gap between these students and their more advantaged peers. Measurable success resulting from this effort can be documented by increased numbers of these students, as well as other students, completing school academically prepared to choose from a wide range of substantial post-secondary options, including college.[16]

EARLY INITIATIVES

The first effort to incorporate student support programs into the national reform agenda recently emerged as a result of the combined efforts of an independent educational policy organization and a large foundation. The Education Trust is a nonprofit agency that has been a major actor in helping to set the broader school reform agenda.[17] The Wallace–Reader's Digest Fund (now reorganized as the Wallace Foundation) has significant funding initiatives focused on strengthening schools and communities.[18] The origins of the Transforming School Counseling Initiative (TSCI)—outside of the professional association and the major national school reform policy players—is an indicator of how low the profile of the student support professional has been over the past few decades.

The assumption underlying the Wallace Foundation–Education Trust TSCI effort was the recognition that the continuing emphasis of within-school student support on fostering psychosocial adjustment has become untenable. This reality is the product of two intersecting pressures that have been transforming American public schools for some 25 years. The first pressure is demographic and is reflected in the current student population, which is, particularly in urban areas, increasingly poor, minority, or composed of recent immigrants. These students' needs cannot possibly be met by a few school-based counselors and social workers, and the increasing demands for social services are best addressed by better-funded and more comprehensive community agencies. The second pressure is a shift in policy that places increasing accountability on teachers and administrators to improve the performance of all students. The primary focus of schools is, after all, on cognitive development and preparation for adulthood. School counselors have drifted from this focus, but their training in human development and experience in school settings make them a potentially powerful resource when harnessed to concrete educational goals.

While the TSCI program does not explicitly include other professional groups, such as social workers and school psychologists, the thrust of the program's arguments can easily be applied to student support professionals generally. Instead of promoting a comprehensive guidance program, we introduced at the beginning of this chapter the idea of a comprehensive support program (CSP) that includes not only counselors, but also all the other key student support players. We will revisit this concept later in the chapter and develop the CSP idea throughout this book.

Patricia Martin, whose background work set the agenda for the TSCI initiative, asserts that "change for school counseling is not optional—it is mandatory for school counseling to survive in the rapidly changing environment of K–12 schools."[19] With the drive for educational reform that involves measurable performance and increased student achievement, the need for counselors to link their roles with the new reform is imperative. Martin argues that "professionals who do not add to this bottom line are considered superfluous to schools."[20]

Martin's major message to the field of student counseling is that improving academic achievement is missing from the official duties of most practicing school counselors. In the current reform climate, this inevitably puts them at the sidelines. The Wallace Foundation and the Education Trust envision a new role for counselors, which includes providing leadership in schools, advocating for students, working as a core member of school improvement teams, and providing essential support through the analysis and assessment of student data. To complement these goals, the TSCI focuses on altering the training counselors receive to prepare them for new roles that go beyond tracking and recording student tests to more actively interpreting student performance data and developing strategies to encourage academic success.

The Wallace Foundation's focus is on changing preparation programs in universities rather than on reaching practicing counselors.[21] The impact of the TSCI on schools in the short run has, therefore, been intentionally limited. It has been controversial as well because it seemed to be rejecting a core assumption of most school counselors, which stressed the importance of mental health as a foundation for personal development. At the same time that the TSCI was being proposed, some influential members of the profession argued that real transformation meant reemphasizing the mental health needs of adolescents.[22] These conflicting messages continue to stimulate debate in the field of school counseling.

The American School Counseling Association (ASCA) incorporated the reform ideas from the TSCI and expanded them to produce a national model for school counseling reform. We argue that the ASCA model is the best one available for a glimpse into the work being done in the professional sphere on transforming the roles of school counselors. The model does not incorporate all student social service professionals, but the dimensions included in it are equally important and relevant to all student support staff.

The ASCA model built on the TSCI to create a practical framework for school counselors to implement in their districts and schools. ASCA adopted the Education Trust's ideas of the counselor as *leader, advocate,* and *collaborator,* and expanded them to fit into a broader, more comprehensive new model of student support. The following is an excerpt from a 1997 summary of how ASCA leaders viewed the new purpose of school counseling:

> The purpose of a counseling program in a school setting is to promote and enhance the learning process. The goal of the program is to enable all students to achieve success in school and to develop into contributing members of our society. A school counseling program based on national standards provides all the necessary elements for students to achieve success in school. This programmatic approach helps school counselors to continuously assess their students' needs, identify the barriers and obstacles that may be hindering success, and advocate programmatic efforts to eliminate these barriers.[23]

Judy Bowers and Trish Hatch developed the new national ASCA model by researching the history of school guidance and by collecting and analyzing data, state documents, and interviews. According to them, "The purpose of ASCA's National Model . . . is to create one vision and one voice for school counseling programs."[24] The ASCA framework encourages school counselors to focus not only on the high-achieving or the high-risk students, but *all* students. The model also encourages collaboration between counselors and teachers, outside sources, and the administrative staff. In addition, ASCA encourages counselors to monitor student progress using data-driven leadership. The following quotation, from a counseling services coordinator whom we interviewed, exemplifies the emerging ideas of new-vision counseling:

One of my counselors is not really backing the terms of where we're going. She's very good at what she does and she also has very good mental-health skills. She wants to do the groups herself, she wants to see her kids, she wants to do her developmental guidance activities. She called me the day after the Columbine tragedy and said, "Laurel, see, if we go through with the SOAR [a TSCI new-vision reform model] initiative like you're talking about, I wouldn't have been able to have been out in my classrooms today, meeting with my kids who needed my help." I said, "Alice, how many classrooms did you get to today?" She got to four. I said, "How many do you have in the school?" They had 18. I said, "How many kids did you get to talk with, one-on-one?" She got to talk to six or something like that, briefly. I said, "What if you had a team of parents who were trained in crisis management and, when a crisis occurred, you called them that night and they came to the school and you briefed them and you all went out? You would still get to see those six kids, but now all of your school has been served." I said, "That is SOAR. It doesn't take away from what you're doing. It just adds to it. You can still do that, if that's the way you want to handle it. You can train all your volunteers to do it and you could be the administrator if you don't want to do it. That's SOAR. It doesn't mean those kids aren't going to get those services. It means that we make better use of our resources so that when they need the personal-social, we're there for them too." So, anyway, she did have to take a step back on that. "Well, I don't know if I can train my parents to do that," she said. It's hard for her to let go.

This quotation represents one of the major tenets of the ASCA model—that school counselors should reach *all* students in the school through a reorganization of services.

According to the ASCA model, the new vision of school counseling includes descriptors that are foreign to the old model, such as *leadership, advocacy,* and *data-driven decision making.* We argue that these descriptors are also the template to integrate the functions of student support professionals with the teaching staff to promote common educational improvement goals.

How Do Student Support Professionals Become Leaders in Your School?

The first step in turning support staff into school leaders is not to ignore them. This means involving student support professionals on leadership teams in your school to help make systemic changes and decisions on behalf of all student needs. The principal as change master creates a structure of distributed leadership that devolves authority and accountability throughout the school. This process is already underway in many schools among the teaching staff, and the ASCA model extends this to the entire professional staff within the school.

How Do Student Support Professionals Become Advocates?

Student support professionals become advocates for students by providing them with the necessary resources they need to succeed—in graduating and in life after graduation. They become advocates for teachers when they work collaboratively with teachers to get the whole picture of the student and partner with teachers in increasing student achievement. They become school advocates by communicating directly with parents to create home-school partnerships for their children's best interests.

What Does It Mean for Student Support Professionals to Be Data-Driven?

According to the ASCA National Model, data-driven decision making involves the following:

- **Using Data.** "The use of data to effect change within the school system is integral to ensuring that every student receives the benefits of the school [support] program. Student support professionals must show that each activity implemented as part of the program was developed from a careful analysis of students' needs, achievement and related data."[25]
- **Monitoring Students.** "Monitoring students' progress ensures all students receive what they need to achieve success in school. It entails monitoring student achievement data, achievement-related data, and standards- and competency-related data. Collection, analysis and interpretation of student achievement data may be systemic by district or specific to school site, grade, class or individual."[26]
- **Closing the Gap.** The "gap" we refer to is defined as the discrepancy between desired results and the current level of achievement. The use of data will drive the program. Data is used to assess where the student support program is now and where it should go. Needs will surface when disaggregated data are analyzed for every student.

In addition to the above descriptors, the ASCA National Model also includes the following concepts:

- **Collaboration/Teaming.** Collaboration includes not only teaming with teachers and outside sources, but also with all student support professionals. One way for teachers and student support personnel to collaborate is by team-teaching on such subjects as career exploration and study skills training.

- **Counseling/Coordinating.** This includes coordinating tasks with teachers and all student support staff as well as small- and large-group counseling around various social and academic-related themes.

THE ROLE OF THE ADMINISTRATOR IN THE ASCA NATIONAL MODEL

Not surprisingly, the ASCA National Model emphasizes the role of school counselors as the agents of change for their own professional practice. However, ASCA also recognizes that the role of the administrator is central:

> Administrators provide support for the organization, development and implementation of the school counseling program. They encourage counselors and teachers to work cooperatively and allow time, facilities and resources to facilitate the process. The administrator recognizes and supports school personnel and community members' important roles in the implementation of the school counseling programs.[27]

ASCA believes that administrator support is necessary for the successful implementation of the new model. All school counseling staff, in addition to the administrator in charge of the school counseling department, must collaborate to make effective management decisions. According to the ASCA framework, principals and administrators are involved in this process for the following important reasons:

1. Administrators are the school leaders who understand the school's direction and needs.

2. Administrators who meet regularly with the counseling staff to discuss the school's mission and the counseling program are critical links in supporting the school's mission and meeting student needs.

3. Without administrator support, school counseling programs may strive, but they will not thrive.

4. An involved and supportive administrator is one of the school counseling program's best advocacy tools.

5. Administrators can work collaboratively with counselors to create a systemic and interdependent approach to improve student academic achievement.

6. Both school counselors and administrators are responsible for the needs of every student, especially those who are under-served.[28]

Administrators clearly play an essential role in helping counselors and other student support professionals become leaders in the school. The next section outlines the core functions of student support staff as an introduction for organizing and coordinating student support roles.

STUDENT SUPPORT FUNCTIONS

The ASCA model posits three functions as the foundation for all student support roles:

1. Academic Assistance

2. Career Counseling (i.e., life planning after school)

3. Personal and Social Support

We would add a fourth function for the typical high school:

4. Linkage With Community Service Agencies

These functions can be divided among your student support staff depending on the needs of your school and the capabilities of your student support team. As we stated in Chapter 1, distributive leadership stresses analyzing organizational needs and the functions associated with those needs, instead of focusing on individual roles. This means you must first identify the functions necessary to a successful school, and *then* assess your staff strengths in each functional area. The ASCA model is a framework to conceptualize how the functions of the entire student support staff can be expanded and intertwined.

Central to the model is linking student support functions to broader state and national standards. The following is a list of student competencies, outlined by ASCA, that define the knowledge, attitudes, or skills students should obtain or demonstrate as a result of participating in a school counseling program:

Academic Development
A. Students will acquire the attitudes, knowledge, and skills contributing to effective learning in school and across their lifespan.
B. Students will complete school with the academic preparation essential to choose from a wide range of substantial postsecondary options, including college.

C. Students will understand the relationship of academics to the world of work and to life at home and in the community.

Career Development

A. Students will acquire the skills to investigate the world of work in relation to knowledge of self and to make informed career decisions.
B. Students will employ strategies to achieve future career goals with success and satisfaction.
C. Students will understand the relationship between personal qualities, education, training, and the world of work.

Personal/Social Development

A. Students will acquire the knowledge, attitudes, and interpersonal skills to help them understand and respect themselves and others.
B. Students will make decisions, set goals, and take necessary action to achieve goals.
C. Students will understand safety and survival skills.[29]

Schools cannot take on the burden for ameliorating conditions in the wider community. Nonetheless, because schools see large numbers of children for long periods of time, they are ideal settings in which to identify the conditions in a student's life that interfere with learning. We do not believe that most schools are suitable sites for delivering nonacademic services and we agree with ASCA that providing linkages to social services should not be a major role for school counselors. However, in many schools, there is a pressing need to make use of community agencies that provide services directly related to getting students ready to learn. In many schools, social workers handle these triage and referral functions. Where there are no social workers, someone else within the school—a nurse, vice principal, or even a specialized counselor—will take on these responsibilities. We would, therefore, add the following goals to the ASCA model:

Community Engagement

A. Students will have access to one or more individuals who are knowledgeable about community social services.
B. Schools will be linked to appropriate community services that have the responsibility to ensure that they are safe, housed, and healthy—and therefore ready to learn.

In order to meet these guidelines, we suggest that student support personnel work with the principal to create a working list of activities required for reaching these goals. But, unless counselors and other student support professionals let go of traditional tasks and attitudes, they will never have the time, ability, or inclination to move in a new direction. Table 2.1 outlines the difference between counseling activities and noncounseling activities, as

Table 2.1   ASCA Chart of Counseling Duties

Counseling Duties	Noncounseling Duties
• Planning individual student academic programs	• Registration and scheduling of all new students
• Interpreting cognitive, aptitude, and achievement tests	• Coordinating or administering cognitive, aptitude, and achievement tests
• Counseling students who are tardy or absent	• Signing excuses for students who are tardy or absent
• Counseling students who have disciplinary problems	• Performing disciplinary actions
• Counseling students as to appropriate school dress	• Sending students home who are not appropriately dressed
• Collaborating with teachers to present guidance curriculum lessons	• Teaching classes when teachers are absent
• Analyzing grade point averages in relationship to achievement	• Computing grade point averages
• Interpreting student records	• Maintaining student records
• Providing teachers with suggestions for better management of study skills	• Supervising study halls
• Ensuring that student records are maintained as per state and federal regulations	• Keeping clerical records
• Assisting the school principal with identifying and resolving student issues, needs, and problems	• Assisting with duties in the principal's office
• Working with students to provide small- and large-group counseling services	• Working with one student at a time in a therapeutic, clinical mode
• Advocating for students at individual education plan meetings, student study teams, and school attendance review boards	• Preparing individual education plans, student study teams, and school attendance review boards
• Analyzing disaggregated data	• Entering data

SOURCE: Adapted from Campbell & Dahir (1997). Used with permission.

viewed by the ASCA model. This chart can help you as a change master identify the difference between what counselors are typically assigned to do in schools, and how these duties can be shifted or eliminated altogether.

The guidelines in Table 2.1 were written with only school counselors in mind, but the ASCA purpose of creating integration with overall school structures and goals expands easily and naturally to encompass all student support personnel. Therefore, we propose that the three functions of academic advising, career counseling, and personal/social support form the core goals for student support professionals—whether they are social workers, chemical dependency counselors, or college advisors—and that our fourth category, community engagement, be incorporated as a shared responsibility between school administration and all student support professionals.

FORMING A COMPREHENSIVE SUPPORT PROGRAM

Earlier in this chapter, we introduced the idea of a CSP or department that coordinates all student support functions around the four core areas discussed above. Much like a team model, a CSP can include teams of student support staff conducting study skills groups, time management trainings, classroom units aimed at improving test skills, assessing target groups of children, and achievement motivation groups, to name a few.[30] In addition, CSP personnel may reach out to parents and offer classes that teach them how to support their children academically. Creating a CSP team is one way for these staff to become involved in all four focus areas: academics, career planning, personal/social support, and community engagement. But, the school's change master—you—must incorporate these functions into their new vision. Communication among all student support professionals in the school is essential to reducing overlap of functioning as well as incidences of students falling through the cracks.

One of the major problems with reorganizing student support functions in schools is the silo attitudes and behaviors of some student support professionals. Even with the best of intentions, student support professionals in large urban schools often lack the time or energy to effectively coordinate with other student support professionals. In many cases, social workers are more fragmented in their job functions than school counselors. The following is a real-life example of how a school with plenty of resources can function poorly because of issues with coordination of services and especially communication.

Resource Rich, Organizationally Deficient: An Example

South Central School District is in a semi-rural area only a little over an hour away from a major city. The town has fallen on hard times in the last 25 years: Large Victorian houses on its main street belie an underlying poverty that is reflected in the high school population, which is 35% Hispanic, 50% African American, and 15% white. Located in a state that mandates significant staff resources to support special education students, and in a district that has chosen to augment state requirements, South Central High appears lucky: 950 students are served by 5 guidance counselors, 4.5 social workers (3 with master's degrees in social work [MSW] and 1.5 bachelor degrees in social work [BSW]), a substance abuse counselor (SAC), a half-time nurse practitioner, a full-time school nurse, and a learning consultant. A single school psychologist serves the entire district, which also includes K–8 schools.

In spite of the enviable staffing ratio, all are stretched thin. Seen through the eyes of Sherry, the newest MSW, student support seems chaotic. Sherry was hired by the district four years ago as a Home and Health Services Coordinator, "but that was a title, and not the practice." She was told that the focus of her efforts would be on the 65% of the high school students who were not in special education, and that she would work closely with the Health Center located in the building. That focus was immediately undermined when the state cited the school for inadequate "related services" to special education students. According to Sherry, the MSW assigned to the special education diagnostic team is required to complete all of the paperwork associated with the individual educational plan (IEP) process—in order to leave the special education teachers and the districtwide psychologist free to provide in-class services—and she thus has too little time to work with students one-on-one, as is required by the state. Sherry immediately acquired a caseload of approximately 70 special education students whom, by law, she needs to meet with twice a month. In addition, in a typical day, she will see up to 10 students—sometimes several at a time—who crowd into her office with problems ranging from immediate homelessness, to pregnancy, to abusive parents. Home visits are rare, although she believes that they are critical, because all of her time is spent dealing with immediate crises.

Sherry wishes that she could coordinate her work with the other social workers and the SAC, because they all end up seeing the same students. She talks about students who take advantage of the system's disorganization by "social worker shopping" and thus end up spending little time in class. But coordination among the social workers and the SAC is informal because of their different job definitions and because they are so busy—they never meet as a group to discuss their work. She interacts even less often with the guidance counselors, whom she views as "protected by the principal" because they are all located centrally in the administrative office suite. She also speaks enviously of the elementary school social workers, who work in partnership with guidance counselors in providing much more extensive in- and out-of-school support for needy students. Still, Sherry plans to "hang in there" until she is 55, because she loves the kids. By then, she thinks that she will be too tired for anything but a private counseling practice.

This example highlights the importance of implementing a comprehensive support program in which student support professionals coordinate services and communicate with one another. In the medical field, doctors, nurses, and social workers share patient knowledge and information with one another on a regular basis. These hospital care professionals make the rounds regularly together so that they all coordinate information and understand the patients' needs. In addition, they hold care conferences so that all medical professionals working with the patients are on the same page and understand the patients on both physical and mental health levels. We propose a similar structure for a CSP, where teachers, administrators, and all student support professionals regularly share information and ideas about the students.

Change masters must address many barriers to implementing a CSP before they start rearranging their student support resources. The exercises in the resource section of this chapter are only a beginning: Chapter 3 will help you as an administrator understand and identify the barriers before, during, and after creating a CSP.

CONCLUSION

The ASCA literature outlines a vision for counselors. However, the ASCA model does not articulate a broader understanding of the principal's role in guiding the school in refocusing attention on student achievement. Our goal is to incorporate the models, literature, and issues surrounding student support programs into broader models of leadership. One problem with both the TSCI and the ASCA model is the slow spread of these initiatives into the broader conversations about school reform. Our research indicates that the literature on school counseling reforms and student support programs has generally not percolated up to the administrative levels that could provide the necessary support for implementation. In addition, we found few articles and references linking these models to comprehensive school reforms.

Because no one profession has a handle on systemic change, we draw on the broader leadership models to help you reorganize your student support team. In Chapter 3, we identify common barriers to reforming student support and student support programs in schools. In Chapter 4, we provide examples of principals who have integrated their student social services successfully. Finally, in Chapters 5 and 6, we introduce the steps you can take to begin this process.

RESOURCES

As a change master, you need to be involved in designing and organizing new models of student support in addition to setting the expectations of what that design can accomplish. What are the things that need to happen in order for your student support staff programs to function at a high level? The following exercises will help you assess the student support needs in your school and find the best way to utilize your student support staff.

Exercise 1. Crisis Prevention:
How to Chart and Assess Your Student
Support Staff Functions Beginning With At-Risk Students

The four overlapping school functions identified earlier—academic advising, personal/social support, career counseling, and community engagement—are the important pieces in student support professionals successfully linking to the overall student achievement agenda. All four of these areas need to be monitored for indicators of success or failure on a regular basis to detect students with precrisis conditions. There are a wide range of behaviors that impinge upon student achievement and those behaviors need to be dealt with in a quick and effective way.

Figure 2.1 outlines how many schools handle day-to-day crises. Typically, student support staff in schools have little time to communicate with their fellow staff members about students in need. In many schools, crisis intervention takes up much of the student support staff's time and effort throughout the day.

Figure 2.1   Typical Support Staff Day-to-Day Response to School Crisis

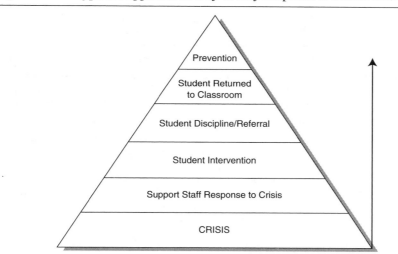

As a principal, the systems you have in place to target students with academic, career, or personal/social issues must be revisited on a regular basis to ensure that every child is accounted for and making progress. The pyramid in Figure 2.2 is an example of how to reorganize your school so that crises do not hijack all of your student support time and energy. It illustrates a system of check-ins to monitor students' academic, career, and personal/social needs by designated staff members on a regular basis so that you, the change master, can hone in on the most important student support issues facing your school on a given day. The purpose of a check-in system is to create a staff dedicated to detecting issues and measuring progress to prevent crisis—not just reacting after it has occurred, as in the South Central High School example. The base of the check-in system is the foundation for the model and incorporates the day-to-day monitoring of student academic, career, and personal/social progress and linking these issues with relevant community linkages.

Figure 2.2 Systemic Prevention of Crisis

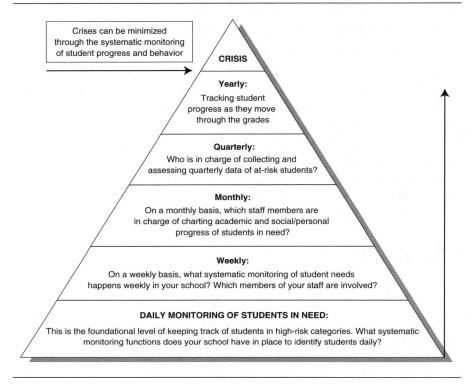

Use Figure 2.2 as a diagnostic tool to help you organize and realign your support system, especially for students who are designated as having special needs in any of the following areas: behavioral, developmental, social, or academic. In Chapter 4, you will see an example of how one principal used a similar pyramid structure to realign his student support staff so that their efforts focus on regularly monitoring behavior and attendance indicators with the ultimate goal of increasing student achievement.

Exercise 2. Assessing Your Current Student Support Resources: What Are Your Student Support Staff Functions Now in Your School?

What are your current daily, weekly, monthly, and yearly student support staff activities for monitoring students? Who are the designated school professionals assigned to monitor these function areas? Our research indicates that not all principals are aware of what their student support staff do on a daily, monthly, or even yearly basis. We identified a few extreme examples of principals who had no idea what their student support professionals did, except in a very vague way.

Use the chart in Table 2.2 as a starting point for filling in what each support professional's duties are in your school. You can begin by thinking of the kinds of mechanisms student support staff have in place for students considered to be at-risk, and then use the chart again to fill in how the rest of the students in school are monitored. Begin by asking yourself and your staff the following: "In our school, our [specify guidance, social work, etc. staff] does [what?] on a [daily, weekly, monthly, yearly] basis to monitor student

Table 2.2   Map of Student Support Functions

	Daily Monitoring	Weekly Monitoring	Monthly Monitoring	Quarterly Monitoring	Yearly Monitoring
Academic					
Tasks that link to academic achievement					
Designated school/outside professionals in charge of tasks					
Mechanisms that support communication about academic progress to other staff members					
Career					
Tasks that link to student life after high school					
Designated school/outside professionals in charge of tasks					
Mechanisms that support communication about college/ career/life plan progress to other staff members					
Social/Personal					
Tasks that link to social/ personal health					

(Continued)

Table 2.2 (Continued)

	Daily Monitoring	Weekly Monitoring	Monthly Monitoring	Quarterly Monitoring	Yearly Monitoring
Designated school/outside professionals in charge of tasks					
Mechanisms that support communication about the social/personal health of students to other staff members					
Community Engagement					
Tasks that link schools to community					
Designated school/outside professionals in charge of tasks					
Mechanisms that support communication and linkages between school and community					

[academic, career, personal/social] progress." Then, fill in Table 2.2 with the answers. This will create a map of your current system so that you can identify holes that need to be addressed immediately.

After identifying how your student support staff functions in the schools, discuss ideas on how they might better communicate and coordinate with one another. You can use this chart as a tool to help your staff create additional tasks and strategies to identify students' needs and to anticipate where and when your support staff, teachers, and other professionals should successfully transfer student knowledge and data. The ASCA chart of appropriate duties of school guidance personnel shown earlier in the chapter may come in handy for an initial analysis of your situation. After filling out Table 2.2, you can begin to set up an intervention system—such as the one outlined in Figure 2.2—so that the entire school staff can stay abreast of the successes or problems of individual students. Remember, newer models of student support also emphasize that all students should be helped by student support; therefore, if your staff are only focused on visibly needy students, then more than likely there are students out there desperately in need of academic, personal/social, and career support who are not being served.

This chart you create using Table 2.2 is a stepping stone for redesigning your student support functions to more closely match the needs of students. We suggest that you create a new chart and pyramid based on specific targeted areas, such as attendance, behavior, or progress on an ongoing testing regimen. This will help you, as a change master, to map out what you currently have in place at your school, and it will highlight areas that are not being adequately covered. Remember, if there is a hole in your map, there will be a student who will find a way to fall into it.

Sample Job Description for School Social Worker

The following real job description (with information that would permit identifying the district from which it comes removed) illustrates the broad expectations from districts and schools for student support professionals. As you will see, some of the functions listed below involve new-model student support tasks, such as serving on a leadership team and communicating effectively with other staff members. Yet many of the tasks also fit into the old-model vision of student support where social workers and others are expected to provide "duties as assigned."

Social Worker Job Description: Essential Functions

1. Provide or obtain counseling services for students and their families.

2. Identify special needs of students and families and refer to appropriate resources.

3. Prepare and interpret social and developmental histories and assessments.

4. Help ensure participation of parents in school conferences affecting their children through home visits, telephone, correspondence, or other means.

5. Help ensure parents' understanding of decisions, procedures, and meetings affecting their children.

6. Participate in special education evaluations and staffing, as necessary, to help ensure continuity of the educational program, and facilitate parent involvement.

7. Provide mediation services to resolve conflicts involving the school and the parents or students.

8. Serve as liaison between the school, parents, and community agencies to coordinate case services.

9. Assist in the development of services to address unmet needs of students and their families, when such needs impair students' school adjustment or ability to receive maximum benefit from school experience.

10. Provide consultation to school and community agencies to increase students' benefits from the school program.

11. Provide and participate in staff development and inservice training programs.

12. Participate in special education placement staffing, when appropriate.

13. Serve as an advocate for parents to help ensure that their wishes and concerns regarding their children are made known to personnel in schools and community agencies.

14. Participate in evaluation of the effectiveness of programs and services.

15. Serve as a representative for the schools on community or special education panels, groups, etc., when requested and appropriate.

16. Provide supervision work for field-placement students.

17. Participate in preschool screenings as needed.

18. Perform other such social work functions related to the school program as appropriate.

19. Secure appropriate services for exceptional students referred by school Child Find teams, special education leaders, school psychologist, school personnel, and others.

20. Provide and maintain adequate communication with school and staff personnel relative to the needs of exceptional students.

21. Establish and maintain continuing professional relationships with community and social agencies.

22. Use effective positive interpersonal communication skills.

23. Perform other incidental tasks or services consistent with the job goal of this position.

24. Use appropriate techniques and strategies that promote and enhance critical, creative, and evaluative thinking of students.

25. Use appropriate instruction strategies and materials that reflect each student's culture, learning styles, special needs, and socioeconomic background.

26. Fulfill the terms of any affected written contract and adhere to the Codes of Ethics and Principles of Professional Conduct of the Education Profession of State X.

27. Assist in the enforcement of all federal, state, and district regulations, policies, and procedures.

28. Monitor students in a testing environment.

29. Provide outstanding customer service, and use positive interpersonal communication skills.

30. Make all decisions and perform all tasks in accordance with District Y Public Schools Organizational Values.

31. Ensure compliance with board rules and applicable federal laws and regulations.

32. Perform tasks or services consistent with the job goal of this position.

Barriers to Creating **3** a Comprehensive Support Program

> In this chapter you will
>
> - Learn to recognize barriers that impede your efforts to reorganize your student support team.
> - Learn about successful ways of removing barriers without hindering the overall process.
> - Acquire ideas on how to change student support roles to better align them with your school's mission.

As we stated in previous chapters, counselors and other student support personnel have been backbenchers in the ongoing drama of school reform. Their contact with students or parents is usually brief, and teachers have only a vague idea of what they do. In most current systems, it is the students who are in trouble that are most likely to find their way to the counselor's or social worker's office, where resources to help them are often limited. The typical counselor who spends his or her days on 10-minute guidance sessions and putting out fires has little time and no structural mechanisms in place to work on removing barriers to student learning.

In this chapter, we will look at how student support professionals are currently being used in schools and compare that reality with the new models we introduced in Chapter 2. Our research has primarily focused on the role of the school counselor, but our goal is to embrace all student support personnel into your 10% solution in order to create a comprehensive support program.

AUTHORS' NOTE: The authors wish to thank Heidi Barajas, Pat Seppanen, and Dan Pepper, who worked on earlier analyses for this chapter.

There is no simple explanation for why counselors, social workers, and other student support professionals have been largely overlooked in the successive waves of school reform. Schools are difficult to change, not because the people in them are resistant (although they sometimes are), but because every good idea requires rearranging many interconnected parts in the organizational puzzle. This chapter will look at how student support roles have evolved into their current form, and we will provide evidence of what changes are required if new models of student support are to take root.

CHANGING THE ROLE OF STUDENT SUPPORT PROFESSIONALS

Our perspective is drawn from our own research in seven school districts (referred to in the Appendix) as well as others' experience with recent systemic change initiatives. Change is always difficult, and an attempt to reinvigorate the role of student support personnel in K–12 educational institutions meets the same kinds of impediments as other current reform efforts. Schools are designed to operate as stable organizations whose processes and outcomes are predictable for everyone involved: teachers, administrators, students, and the public. Administrators know that they must support the persistence of habits and structures that appear to have served well in the past, even as they urge people to keep up with the pressures to change.[1] In critical social institutions, such as schools, a preference for stability is part of protecting children and families from untested theories or practices—just as hospitalized patients are reassured by established treatment protocols. Change occurs slowly, as organizations recognize repetitive problems, make decisions about emerging policies and practices, and calculate how best to achieve new objectives. While some school critics demand "transformation" or "reengineering," radical change in schools is rarely supported by the public, which approaches new and even well-researched ideas cautiously.

Reasonable public concerns about the consequences of radical reform are supported by the internal organization of schools, which is usually hierarchical with clear divisions of labor. Superintendents and their staff carry out broad policy directions, and principals are the on-site supervisors who guide the work of teachers, students, and support staff.[2] While teachers have considerable autonomy in carrying out their daily work, they increasingly follow set patterns of curriculum and school timetables. People know what teachers do: They prepare lessons, engage in instruction, and assess student learning. They are assumed to be leaders in their classroom, within definite administrative constraints. Student support staff are different. In their current form, counselor and social worker jobs are nonrationalized roles within a highly organized setting. Amorphous duties and responsibilities, an unclear location for work, and an emphasis on individualized therapeutic interventions means that most actors in the school system do not associate the student support roles with leadership.[3] We have found that even teachers often misunderstand how student support professionals fit into the school structure.

Student support roles must also be viewed through the lens of school culture.[4] A school's culture consists of values and norms that create assumptions about the "right" way to do things and how to interpret experiences.[5] It is often assumed that a school's culture is monolithic, but any large organization also contains subcultures, and the more unsettled the times, the more likely it is that subcultures will form.[6] When the environment is calm and supportive, it is easy for teachers, student support staff, and parents to see themselves as a unified front in support of children. When there are instability and demands for improvement, formerly cohesive groups may offer solutions with dramatically different perspectives that reveal underlying cultural differences. Any solution that attempts to integrate the function of different professional groups will, at some point, have to address the divergent and stereotypical views they have of each other.

A policy overview is also needed to understand what must change if student support programs are to become an integral part of the reform agenda in schools. Schools are under enormous pressure from state legislatures and national groups to measure and improve their performance— and to do it without increased resources. These pressures create a system of organized anarchy, in which presumably rational decision-making processes are affected by a shifting definition of problems, an array of incompatible solutions, and competing pressure groups. As a consequence, the trajectory of school change is often indirect and only partially manageable.[7]

In this chapter, we use all three perspectives—structural, cultural, and policy—to examine the issues faced by school administrators as they attempt to change the practice and positions of student support professionals in improving academic achievement for all students. Within each of these general categories, we provide examples of the real work of student support in the schools that we have worked with.

THE PROBLEM OF STRUCTURE

The Counselor's Role: One Principal's Perspective

The following is an excerpt from an interview we conducted with a high school principal in a southern state:

I have three full-time counselors and one part-time counselor; next year, I will have four full-time counselors because my projected enrollment goes to 1,864. When you say four counselors to service all the needs, that's very difficult because it's one-on-one. On any given day, you will see that counselors' doors are always open. They are meeting with teachers and students. Teachers come to them with concerns about specific students. They are addressing those concerns. They are meeting with parents throughout the day.

My expectations are very, very high. My counselors divide up the student population by their last name, and they work with those students through the 4-year period of time. I want them to know everything they possibly can about those students, besides their grade history and where they're going to go to college. I want them to try to establish some type of personal rapport with them, so that they can come with their needs, whether they are academic or personal. My expectations are also to make sure that my students are on track for the college seal of endorsement or career tech; that they are on line to graduate at the proper time. So, I expect the grade histories to be up-to-date so that my students know they have the plan of action necessary to meet their goal of graduation and then to go on. I expect my counselors also to keep documentation of conferences. I want my community involved here at Southeast High School. I want conferences held with students and parents in attendance where they are able to sit down one-on-one and discuss issues about their sons and daughters.

It's very, very important that our counselors are part of our academic program by doing classroom guidance. They are advising them on career aspirations, the sources of information that can be found through different programs that are housed within the school, and they can go and seek information and find out what items are pertinent to their individual needs. Our counselors do presentations about the next level of education, whether that be college, the military, or a technical institution. For example, they introduce the PSAT to all 9th, 10th, and 11th graders on a yearly basis and talk about how the PSAT is an excellent indicator for their career goals. And they help the 9th graders to shore up their weaknesses or to enhance their strengths so that they do well on the PSAT. They go in and talk about the test before it is administered, and, when the results come back, the counselors do a full circle to explain what the score reports indicate, how you read them, and how you can improve from one year to the next. They're also updating transcripts on a daily basis. They are meeting requests of students on doing recommendation forms, sending out transcripts to colleges.

I expect them to be up-to-date with all resources, including all police departments, fire departments, social workers, hospitals, so that they know what agencies need to be involved in order to meet the needs of the students. We have many extended families today. I want them to know who has custody of a child, what procedures they must adhere to, and what can be shared with whom. If we have an emergency where a student is transported to a hospital, a counselor will go with the ambulance. So, I expect them to be the caretaker until the parent takes over. I know that they work with all these agencies at different times in dealing with different situations. For example, my counselors work with social workers that are assigned to our school. And they are, on a daily basis, updated through e-mails or telephone calls on certain students, when a student is with the court system, when a student is with social worker issues.

They are working, on a daily basis, with students that have been hospitalized, making sure that when the student comes back there is an initial conference with the parent and the student and the administrator in order to make sure that everybody is on the same page. They also work with the court system, through the probation officers, on any of our students that are on probation. And the probation officers do a visit to the school that the counselor is involved in where that student is with the judicial system. They, on a daily basis, are returning telephone calls to meet the needs of our parents calling in when a child is sick and any special requests that they have.

They are continuously going to different seminars or meetings to be updated on all of the new [state regulations]. To give you an example, this week, all administrators and all counselors went to a violence prevention seminar in order to review what is happening across the United States in schools where we have students who come on campus and take the lives of others.

THE AMBIGUITY OF STUDENT SUPPORT ROLES

This principal's vision and expectations demonstrate part of the problem that we address. Of course, the principal, who was knowledgeable about new-model counselor roles, would like to have someone on her staff provide all of this support to 450+ students and their families. Any sensible person, however, recognizes that her expectation is unrealistic. Most students in high school never appear on the radar screen of the student support system, few parents are ever contacted, and the counselors and social workers rush from crisis to crisis, doing the best they can without getting too far behind in their paperwork. This problem was illustrated by a day in the life of our hypothetical counselor, Jenna, in Chapter 2, as well as by the real-life case of Sherry, the social worker at South Central School High. Those two vignettes pointed out that there is seldom a system in place in the counselors' or social workers' offices to provide academic support (other than scheduling) for the majority of students.

Another significant structural problem results from the variable and vague expectations that most student support professionals face. Student support exists as an ancillary rather than a core component of K–12 education, with student support having little influence over curriculum development and other kinds of decision making within the school. Busy and isolated, support personnel don't have time or standing to challenge the existing structures and expectations. Data collected from district and school administrators as well as from practicing counselors reveal dynamic differences in the perspectives of what a counselor can and should do during the course of the day. This is the natural result of an unclear job description. In most districts, there is no up-to-date document outlining the role of guidance staff, and even fewer that include elements of a reformed student support vision. As an administrator in a large district notes, "One of the things you asked about . . . was the status of the district's guidance plan. There isn't any."

Unexamined role statements consisting of suggestions and expectations that lack specificity or structure do little to help. Even in a district whose mission statement gives counselors partial responsibility for academic achievement, what actually happens in schools is harder to judge. As one principal noted, "On a day-to-day basis, it is hard to remain true to that mission statement. With a district as large as [as ours], with 18 high schools, you would have potentially 18 different views [about the role]."

As this assertion implies, a practical consequence of poorly defined roles is that student support jobs vary enormously, not only from district to district, but also from school to school. The lack of definition gives student support professionals little recourse to promote a different set of activities from those that are locally assigned. One experienced counselor reported that "When I was first hired . . . as a counselor for [a] middle school, . . . number one on my list of duties, I swear to you, was managing the lockers, helping kids get in the broken lockers." It is easy to question why an individual with an advanced professional degree would accept a role definition such as this, but many feel that they have little choice. According to a supportive administrator in another district, a problem in implementing a new vision for counseling staff and others is that student support personnel usually work alone and are not part of the core academic or administrative team.

Principals and district administrators accept that student support staff operate largely behind the scenes in isolated and unclear roles—and that most student support personnel accept this as well. The director of counseling in a large district suggests that counselors need more than a new role—they need a new set of skills that will permit them to promote a new understanding of their role inside the school: "Before we can demonstrate the new counselor role, we must give the counselors the skills; counselors don't know how to present themselves differently to principals—they don't know how to run a program."

School Administrators as Interpreters of the Student Support Role

The ambiguous role definition provided by districts means that the actual work of student support personnel assigned to a specific school is largely determined by the building administrator. School principals are almost always recruited from the teaching force and have had little exposure to the work of counselors, and their training seldom considers student support programs. Thus, each principal is left to invent a student support department (or, more likely, separate departments for each student support team) and to function with minimal guidance—often based on his or her experience during an internship or in a previous position. While the counselor respondents in our studies indicated that assertive and experienced student support professionals are sometimes able to educate and shape their administrator's definition of counseling, this situation creates uncertainty. For example, one principal felt justified in increasing counselors' involvement in the testing programs, even though he was aware that it might not be the best use of their time:

> At a time of the year, the proficiency tests drive the role and work of school counselors. We're doing sorting of tests and it's time-consuming for counselors. . . . Those activities are critical for students, but it is a counselor who needs to unbox tests and make sure each teacher gets them. There's got to be a better distribution of how that works.

Administrators tend to view certain tasks as critical to student success and a legitimate part of the counselor or social worker role. This occurs because of the beliefs that school administrators and teachers maintain about what student support staff do on a daily basis. Each time a school gets a new principal, the job description needs to be negotiated; the less experienced the principal, the less likely he or she is to know how student support professionals might help students' academic achievement.

As mentioned in Chapter 2, at an extreme, some student support staff become "gofers" who facilitate other school functions between their responsibilities for managing unpredictable student crises. Student support professionals are assigned tasks based on the perception that, because they do not teach classes, they have the flexibility to do multiple duties. For example, the following counselor's remarks show what is valued within the school itself: If one is not engaged in the teaching task, then one's job and time are viewed as less important and more flexible. "In the schools, people say, 'Who is going to do this? Hey, counselors don't have any assigned tasks—let them do it.'"

A middle school counselor described his role as the person who delivers paperwork to the district's payroll office: "I'm the person who is likely asked to go, since I do not have a class." He also assumed new roles that don't clearly belong in anyone else's job description: He is the school's truant coordinator, charged with contacting parents, outside agencies, and the district to inform them of a student's absence. Additionally, his principal assigned him to the role of coordinator of the attendance program. The state requires that students with five unexcused absences within a 30-day period be reported to the district and state attorney's offices. The counselor remarked that "keeping up with that is a major, major problem. About 35 to 40 kids are reported each month under the new law."

So, What Do Student Support Staff Do—or Not Do?

The chart of appropriate duties in Chapter 2 gives an idealized list of counseling and noncounseling duties. In reality, however, most schools are far from implementing the new vision of student support. In a survey that we sent to five different states, we asked over 1,000 practicing counselors how they actually spend their time and what they think they ought to be doing.[8] We analyzed the responses of the practicing school counselors in the survey and came up with the following items that best reflect counselor's priorities and actual allocation of work time. Counselors are quite clear about their priorities, and eight identifiable groups emerged. The two that were viewed as most central were the following:

- **Improving Social Skills** (e.g., decision making, managing emotions, etc.). We asked how important it is to work with students in small groups on personal and social issues. Nearly 50% of respondents indicated that it was "extremely important." This was also the area where counselors spent, on average, the most time. The most commonly reported daily activities were helping students "work on decision-making skills," "manage personal emotions," and "improve interpersonal communication skills."
- **Providing Mental Health Services** (e.g., working on behavioral issues, referring students to mental health services, counseling students individually, etc.). While providing mental health services was an area that more than half of the counselors deemed to be extremely important, relatively few indicated that it was an activity that they engaged in on an almost daily basis.

The other six clusters of activity were regarded as central to the role by fewer respondents. Even where many respondents thought that the role was important, there was often a discrepancy between its rated significance and how their time was actually allocated.

- **Academic and Career Support** (e.g., monitoring student achievement, helping students to identify career goals, developing tutoring and enrichment resources, etc.). Providing academic and career support was considered to be of lower importance by the typical counselor. Only 15% indicated that it was extremely important to use data to identify underperforming students, and about 10% gave a similar priority level to working with students on long-term goals or exploring career interests. These are also activities that few engaged in on a daily basis. For example, only 13% indicated that they worked on helping students with educational and career plans daily, and fewer than 10% felt that they should work with teachers in their classrooms to help students develop long-term goals.

- **Removing Barriers to Achievement** (e.g., working on racial and gender stereotypes, working on study skills, etc.). While approximately 40% of the counselors indicated that activities related to removing achievement barriers were very important, only 6% actually worked with students on study skills on a daily basis. This cluster of activities included many items that reflected concerns about self-esteem and social problems that interfered with achievement, indicating that many counselors see the issues as personal rather than systemic.

- **Advocacy/Change Agent** (e.g., managing the school's bureaucracy, working with teachers and administrators, etc.). Counselors tended to view the cluster of activities related to advocacy as important, but they are, as we shall see, constrained in the degree to which they can enact this role. While most (70%) say that it is "very" or "extremely" important to work with administrators and teachers to improve schools, only 15% see themselves as actively negotiating the school's bureaucracy and fewer (10%) work with teachers on improving the classroom management strategies that might create a healthier learning environment. The survey results also support our contention that counselors are seldom a part of the reform team: Less than 25% of our survey respondents serve on a school governance council, and even fewer work with teachers on curriculum. Their school improvement roles are largely (almost 90%) confined to working with specific problem students and their parents.

- **Organizational Support** (e.g., helping with special education programs, supervising standardized testing, scheduling and planning classes, etc.). Counselors generally believe that administrative tasks are among the least important in their job portfolio. However, as we will show, many of them spend a great deal of time on administrative tasks in addition to scheduling, which is a common administrative activity that is part of most counselors' jobs.

- **Discipline** (working on disciplinary cases). Most counselors—over 50%—have discipline as a daily or frequent component of their work. Few, however, see it as central to their work, and most see their role as counseling students who exhibit behavioral problems (nearly 50% indicate that it is extremely important) rather than developing programs to prevent problems (only 25% report a similar level of importance).

As it turns out, school context makes a great difference in what counselors value and what they do. Counselors in urban schools are far more focused on supporting academic achievement and career planning than those in suburban settings, while counselors in rural or small-town settings spend much less time than their urban and suburban counterparts on developing social and emotional skills. Urban, rural, and small-town counselors spend much more time on discipline than do counselors at suburban high schools. The nature of the student population does not entirely explain these differences: Role definition and the availability of alternative services also affect a counselor's time allocation. For example, the smaller schools in towns and rural areas are unlikely to have an assistant principal whose designated role is to discipline students, while many urban schools struggle with discipline issues due to the high levels of social stress experienced by their students. Perhaps more important, however, these were the only significant differences that could be attributed to location.

There is great variation among counselors in similar types of communities in terms of the priority placed on activities as diverse as social skills training, mental health counseling, college advising, and removing barriers to achievement. The variation that we repeatedly found between counselors in similar communities is explained by the same factors we mentioned in Chapter 1—factors that also answered the question of why counselors and other student support staff have been marginalized in school reform agendas: They have evolved ad hoc without administrative integration with overall school achievement goals.

More significant than school location in predicting a counselor's allocation of time is the age or academic level of the students being served. In order to analyze this issue, we added together the responses that counselors made to the individual questions clustered within each of the eight categories previously described. We discovered that there were significant differences between elementary and secondary counselors in four of these categories. Figure 3.1 shows that the emphasis on career and academic counseling is negligible in elementary school and increases dramatically in middle and high school.

Figure 3.1   Career and Academic Counseling

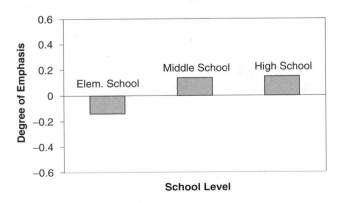

Teachers and parents often complain about increasing inappropriate behavior problems as children get older, and older students clearly face significant behavioral and life decisions. Nevertheless, secondary school counselors place much less emphasis on developing social and decision-making skills among students than do elementary counselors, as is shown in Figure 3.2. Are counselors writing off the possibility of shaping a student's array of social and decision-making skills at the precise time that they are preparing to enter the world as young adults? If so, they are neglecting skills directly related to a student's ability to transition effectively into more complex and less forgiving academic and work environments.

Mental health counseling is also emphasized most in elementary schools, and least in high schools. Middle school counselors emphasize mental health counseling considerably more than do high school counselors, but less than elementary counselors. The similarity between Figures 3.2 and 3.3 leads us to wonder: Are these nonacademic areas crowded out as the

Figure 3.2   Social and Decision-Making Skills

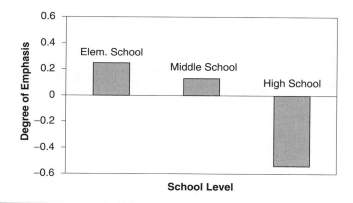

Figure 3.3   Mental Health Counseling

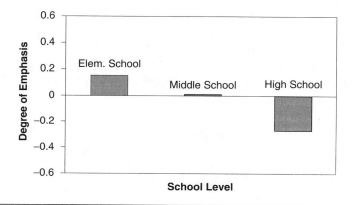

student population ages because of decreasing effectiveness of intervention or is the phenomenon more random than causal? The fact that an organizational explanation is not forthcoming is as relevant as whatever that explanation might be.

Another area in which the role of counselors differed is the emphasis placed on acting as a change agent or advocate working with others to improve the school. Again, we find that elementary school teachers are significantly more likely to see themselves as leaders for change, while middle and high school counselors are less likely to work with other professionals (see Figure 3.4). This may have a simple, structural explanation: There is usually only one counselor in an elementary school, whereas the secondary school counselors work together and are often housed with administrators rather than in proximity to teachers.

Figure 3.4   Working With Others to Change the School

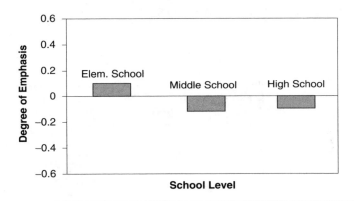

College and career counseling, not surprisingly, is concentrated in high schools—a finding that is so consistent with what we would expect that we do not bother to present the survey figures. There was no significant difference among schools serving elementary, middle, and high schools in three areas: removing barriers to academic achievement, providing organizational support, and discipline. However, these were not among the tasks on which counselors reported spending significant amounts of time.

If we summarize the implications of our limited analysis of the counselor survey, we can point to a number of key issues that deserve a secondary school principal's attention:

1. Practicing school counselors have not fully embraced the reform vision presented in Chapter 2. In general, they view a focus on mental health and individual counseling as most important, and academic support as less important.

2. While secondary school counselors are more likely to emphasize academic and career counseling than are elementary counselors, they are less likely to incorporate an emphasis on student decision-making skills into their work. The new-model student support vision requires that students acquire the skills to make life and academic decisions, and that they be given the necessary information about what classes are required to prepare for graduation or postsecondary education.

3. Counselors, particularly secondary school counselors, rarely see themselves as change agents or members of the school reform team. They are not confident that others see them as leaders.

You can draw one additional conclusion: Unless your school counseling staff is very different from the group that we surveyed, significant effort may be required to create the conditions for a transformed student support team.

School social workers' preferences are also at odds with the expectations of their formal job descriptions, according to a study by Paula Allen-Meares.[9] She found that the tasks socials workers prefer to perform are quite different from those mandated by the state or district, and the school-level tasks that principals expect. She argues that what social workers actually prefer is "more consistent with the needs of pupils and the contemporary challenges facing schools as an institution. However, barriers found within the organization of the school and the administration ofthe school social work services prevent practitioners from focusing on preferred tasks."[10]

Allen-Meares looked at five primary school social worker roles:

1. Leadership and policy making

2. Educational counseling with children

3. Home-school liaison

4. Administrative and professional tasks

5. Facilitating and advocating families' use of community resources

Tasks associated with each of these roles were ranked by social workers. Some of the entry-level tasks viewed as most important emphasized educational counseling and support:

- Acting as advocate for community agencies
- Assessing target groups of children
- Meeting with parents in groups
- Helping develop prevention programs

- Assisting in inservice training of teachers
- Providing information about neighborhoods to administration
- Helping teachers discover children's resources

In contrast, state- and district-mandated tasks included making home visits, referring children and families to community agencies, obtaining information from the children's parents or guardians, and working with each child on an individual basis. Tasks related to leadership and policy making were neither highly ranked by social workers nor expected by states, districts, and principals, which led Allen-Meares to conclude that "social workers, whether entry level or veterans of the field, need to pay more attention to [these] roles and their importance for the achievement of social work goals."[11]

Okay—So, What Needs to Be Done Now?

What does this ambiguity over student support roles mean for secondary school principals and district administrators? We suggest that the fundamental reason that the energy and skills of counselors and other support staff are *not* harnessed to the school reform agenda is that (1) secondary schools are bureaucracies; (2) in bureaucracies—even professional bureaucracies—roles are largely defined by administrators; and (3) the role of student support personnel has evolved to fill voids left by the more clearly enunciated responsibilities of teachers and administrators. In this absence of explicitly designed structures, priorities are set as often by unfolding events as by planning or anticipation. Given the constraints of time and the exigencies of school life, the roles of student support staff have simply not been given the attention that they deserve.

But structure is only one piece of the problem. Although we will provide a number of examples of interesting changes within several student support departments that are promising, changing structures rarely accomplishes a great deal without accompanying changes in people's assumptions and behavior.

THE PROBLEM OF CULTURE

Trying Against the Odds . . .

Jack Partir, principal of an 1,800-student middle school located in a large Western city, came to the school as a counselor in the mid-1990s. He knows what the school's challenges are:

We have 80% language minority students . . . about 50% are classified as English language learners, and about half of those have been in a bilingual program for four or more years. . . . Apartment rentals are cheap here, so people can move in and get one month free, and then move out to get the next best deal.

Mr. Partir struggles to field the services that he knows his students need. His high school has three counselors, one funded by the district and two extra positions funded through a grant. He has many ideas about what could help, but has found that models for counseling services were designed for more tranquil schools than his.

> What everybody's looking for is behavior change. . . . But that is not going to happen immediately. We have to look at ourselves more as an airport or a hotel: People come through us very fast, and we've got to provide a service fairly fast. But a lot of our services aren't effective because [of the transience]. We have students come in, they get involved with the wrong group of kids or decide that they don't like somebody and we have to transfer them out because it's not safe for them to stay here . . . those aren't the conditions for effective counseling interventions.

But, Mr. Partir's problems don't end with a difficult and needy student body. He also has to deal with the adults in the school. His staff often doesn't understand the basic needs of their students' families, and approach their clients with a punitive orientation:

> . . . In most cases, it's not understanding the lack of wealth in this neighborhood. They don't understand that parents don't make appointments because they're walking here, not driving. And, if they've got two or three kids as well and, instead of showing up at 2:00 in the afternoon they show up at 8:00 in the morning, you're not going to send them home—but staff wants to send them home, and tell them to come back. We spend time working with staff about those things, and I spend time talking about how I feel about those things, . . . but I know that a lot of the staff feels that the parents are not as supportive as they should be or as they could be, and that's a big attitude problem.
> I've come to the realization that it's not that the teachers (and some of the counselors) don't know how to [be more student centered], but making a fundamental change is very difficult for anybody to do. There are too many things that are comfortable about the way that they have been doing things. To change any aspect, you have to make other changes. People see that they need to focus on instruction, but don't know how to get out of that [disciplinary] punitive role.

In his efforts to try and change the whole school culture, Mr. Partir has tried professional development, and has made a number of structural changes in an attempt to remove counselors from the first line of discipline. He is torn, however, because he sees counselors as more able to intervene in a caring way—knowing, for example, that a student who comes to school out of uniform is not necessarily flaunting school rules, but may only have one school shirt and no one at home who is attending to laundry. But he feels constrained in his deployment of the counseling staff, which is also traditional in its orientation.

The problems of the surrounding communities are clear, and while the staff in the school tend to blame the culture of poverty, the assumptions and norms of the teachers, counselors, and other student support staff also exacerbate the school's problems.

Teachers' Contributions to Ambiguity

We have described the benign neglect school administrators have shown in creating clear job expectations for counselors and other student support professionals. It is important as well to consider how teachers view the counselors' roles and the assumptions counselors make when they interact with teachers. There is some agreement among counselors that, in general, teachers do not understand how counselors could aid them in student success. One high school teacher observed, "They don't believe guidance does anything for student achievement. At the high school level, they don't understand anything about counseling."

Furthermore, competition exists between counselors and teachers regarding their work effort. Some of this competitive fallout could be attributed to the notion that counselors simply push paper, as illustrated by these comments from counselors:

> You always have a bit of that staff that looks at counselors [and] thinks we don't work as hard as teachers do.

> Counselors have a bad reputation anyway. They [teachers] think we're lazy.

Some teachers and student support staff do see value in collaboration to enable student success. The difficulty is that changing the school's culture to accommodate this emergent relationship requires both parties to think innovatively about their roles and relationships with one another. This requires more than merely redefining the student support job descriptions; it involves changing basic assumptions and attitudes. It is always problematic within a stable bureaucracy to encourage players to drop old responsibilities or acquire new ones. An example would be the multiple changes—in attitude and formal structure—that would be required to have counselors or social workers coach teachers on how to manage problem students within the classroom. A quotation from a counselor illustrates the flip side—counselors acquiring some of the responsibility traditionally left to teachers:

> What will be tricky is changing the mindset. . . . The counselor often defers to the teacher [about a student's assignment to courses]. If we always keep the child at the same level of opportunity, the child will never reach the next level. The counselor has a role to play there.

Teachers often view counselors as the school's disciplinarians and rely on them to manage student problems—outside the classroom. Consistently across sites, counselors stated that teachers often send "problem students" to them for discipline. Counselors, in turn, support the teachers' view by how they handled the students referred to their offices:

> These are students not prepared for class. [They] don't want to conform to rules and regulations. I go a step further—when I get them down here, I use whatever resources I have to encourage them to change.

An individual in another district corroborated this observation, suggesting that "middle schools are a real challenge because they use school counselors as [disciplinarians]."

Teachers perceive counselors not only as necessary for student discipline, but, like many administrators, as social workers to families as well. One counselor said,

> They see me as the mediator and liaison with difficult families. . . . Now, they look to me as far as attendance is concerned because we started an attendance program last year and basically that's my deal, . . . although that is not necessarily something I'm supposed to be doing anything with.

More often than not, the culture of the school insulates the typical teacher from responsibilities in managing individual student problems that fall outside of a clearly defined norm. Student support staff members don't feel free to push back and ask teachers to be more answerable for developing the whole child. Since few support staff see themselves as change agents, they are equally unlikely to question the unstated assumption that the counselor's and other support staff offices are places where all of the school's human problems are solved. If student support personnel are to partner with teachers to make students successful, they will need to take the initiative to change some shared cultural assumptions.

This shift is one for which practicing counselors and social workers have not been prepared.

Moving Away From Mental Health: Where Does Individual Counseling Fit In?

Counselors' expectations need to change in areas other than an increased focus on teachers and the classroom. Student support personnel have their own culture, which reinforces a dichotomy between the academic and the social arenas. As mentioned in Chapter 2, practicing school counselors received their preparation in university programs where many, if not all, of their courses are taken with people training to be family and individual therapists. In fact, not only do teachers and administrators often expect counselors to be mental health therapists, but many counselors also accept this as part of their job. Because of the emphasis on mental health in their training, they enjoy the individual counseling, and most have no desire to change this part of their work. It is not surprising that this is where many counselors wish to devote a large part of their time:

> Fifty percent of [my] week is for individual counseling, which takes most of my time among other activities. . . . I think elementary counselors have more time to do individual counseling.

> It [counseling students individually] is one of our favorite things to do—so we tend to do it, we like to do it.

Left to their own devices and with resources at hand, most counselors are content to work primarily on mental health in one-on-one settings or in small groups. They are often frustrated with the mix of their assigned duties, but view their central responsibility as therapeutic in nature. These counselor remarks are typical:

> Being able to develop the relationship with the parent and to be able to almost work in therapy with the family itself [gives me the greatest satisfaction], and that's very difficult to do in a short time.

> The hardest thing is to accept change, and probably most of us were trained to do a more social work type of counseling—dealing with behaviors with the children. Now that perspective has changed to be academic advisors.

A number of counselors took exception to the idea that they should be more deeply involved in supporting student achievement, noting that it was their job to be student centered and deal with the underlying personal barriers. This attitude often underlies job expectations and a division of labor in which teachers assume responsibility for academic achievement and student support personnel deal with behavioral and emotional issues. One counselor expressed his resistance to change with this observation:

> I don't hear as much as I would like to hear about counseling individuals, counseling meeting the personal needs of kids. I hear the need to do more guidance, advisement, and career work, some of the bigger and broader things, but [that work] is not as much student centered as I'd like to see it.

Others point out that it is difficult, in practice, for counselors to separate the personal and social issues that prevent students from achieving more at school:

> I just got finished talking with a little girl . . . that is living by herself. She's 18. She has an alcoholic uncle who's there occasionally. But when he's there, she usually has to go to a neighbor's. She has . . . an ex-boyfriend who's threatening to kill her. He hits her. He waits in the parking lot and tries to run over her with his truck. And she wants to graduate.

The pressures to maintain an emphasis on clinical counseling come from many other sources as well, and are reinforced when crises occur that upset students. In one school, it is the principal who believes that the role of the counselor includes mental health counseling:

> I would like to see [this counselor], his part of the alphabet, at least be able to schedule every child, maybe once or even twice during the year, to do individual counseling. But, see, the individual counseling that's going on now are the walk-ins in terms of the problems that they're having . . . or they're contacted by the parents and say, "Hey, you need to talk with my son or my daughter this morning." That's the type of individual counseling that is taking place now.

A suicide at one high school in our study stirred a public outcry about counselors who were not sufficiently involved in the individual lives of students:

> It got quoted in the paper over and over and over. . . . High schools were devastated by that comment, because it came out as our counselors don't work with kids.

Parent and student expectations press counselors toward a therapeutic role as well:

> They [parents] view us more as an agency counselor to help with their individual problems. They just walk in. They won't call. It's like a walk-in service and they're sitting here, saying, "This is my problem. . . ."

Not all counselors are in favor of preserving the status quo. Another observed how the one-on-one activities prevent counselors from taking on other important tasks:

> We are usually working with kids all the time. It is direct service to students versus some of the other kinds of things you have to do. We spend very little time in feedback with teachers and parents, working through the principal here. We see kids back-to-back, as many as we can in our time frame.

Principals, even those who believe that student support should focus on academic achievement, see counselors as the front line for managing distraught or angry parents. Whether crisis counseling, social work interventions, or working with families, therapeutic sessions limit the time counselors and social workers have to spend in other duties. Since no one is seriously challenging the current culture, a frequently proposed solution is to hire additional student support personnel rather than change the role of the school counselor and other student support professionals.

The stakeholders in schools fail to agree on an appropriate role for the school student support professionals due, in part, to a lack of an articulate, clear job description at the district level. Practicing school support staff members are rarely guided by a coherent and integrated philosophy of their roles and goals. As a result, they conform to the beliefs and attitudes that prevail in the school—beliefs and attitudes that may only tangentially contribute to the academic success of all students. The lack of a coherent vision results in variable interpretations of student support responsibilities by principals, district administrators, parents, and the students themselves. As if by default, however, our analysis of old-model student support in traditional roles revealed that, across the field, the dominant activities centered on administrative support/paperwork and mental health activities. Both are perceived by most respondents to be important, but they stand in stark contrast with the tasks of new student support models outlined in Chapter 2, which propose realigning student support work around student achievement.

THE PROBLEM OF POLICY[12]

Life Happens

In one district, a local university planned to collaborate with an innovative pilot project already underway. The project, known as the Urban Academy, consisted of two elementary schools and proposed middle and high school sites that were to serve as laboratories in which teams of teachers, principals, and counselors from other schools could come to study ways to improve their own instruction and student achievement in their buildings. School teams of five or six, including a counselor chosen by the faculty, were to spend up to five weeks at the Urban Academy learning, with the help of university faculty, to become leaders of reform in their own buildings. The original idea included the development of an exemplary school counselor professional development program, in which counselors visiting the Urban Academy would observe and learn how to use data, influence system change, broker community services, and collaborate with teachers.

The district superintendent was committed to distributed leadership and had a long-range reform agenda focused on developing the district's human resources. Unfortunately, this was offset by a coordinator of guidance programs who regarded existing counselor arrangements as satisfactory and did not share the superintendent's enthusiasm.

The pilot project experienced several setbacks in its first year. The Urban Academy was slow in getting off the ground and didn't provide the professional development site that practicing counselors and the university had sought. The superintendent, whose long-term vision was not matched by short-term increases in state test scores, was terminated; the Urban Academy was a low priority for the new superintendent, who faced unrelenting pressure to get scores up quickly. By the end of the second year, it was clear that a demonstration professional development site would not emerge, and, except for a handful of committed individuals, the goal of bringing counselors more fully into the reform agenda had faded into the background.

Tugging at Coattails: Getting Policy Attention

Over a decade ago, the College Board concluded that school counselors were reactive rather than proactive. They have historically functioned to help sort students into educational groups determined by policy or common practice, rather than as student advocates in the education system.[13] We have noted that the reasons for this are structural and cultural, but the College Board report also identified another reason that is particularly relevant in light of current school reform efforts: Counselors and other support staff are rarely held accountable for student achievement or how outcomes vary as a function of the race/ethnicity, gender, or socioeconomic status of the student. Furthermore, few student support personnel make use of other available school and community services in order to create a network through which students can be referred for a variety of needs that support personnel, alone, cannot effectively address. There are some initiatives providing incentives for teachers who are particularly effective in promoting achievement among their students, although most of the emphasis of the reform movement has been on holding schools and districts accountable. The emphasis is on teamwork to get results—but counselors and other student support personnel are seldom on the team.

Understanding the role of school counselors in the seven large districts that we studied requires considering how they are viewed both at the district level and in the schools. The seven districts we studied are complicated organizations with countless problems to solve, of which improved deployment of counselors is only one. The standard operating procedures and priorities of urban districts often fail to support the implementation of reformed counselor roles, not through lack of good will, but because of other events and distractions. One district administrator described the effects of a policy vacuum at the district level that contributes to the inability to change the counselor's role at the local level: "I think a lot of it's going to be tradition in practice and roles that limit us more." In his view, the problem is not bureaucratic policy, but the lack of policy.

District leadership is particularly problematic for counselors because of the vague definition of what counselors do and how important they are:

> The leadership on the district side [i.e., a new superintendent] I think is very weak. It's very willing, but does not do a lot of following through, and the leadership actually has come from the field counselors. That's exactly right: It's actually coming from them with no interference from the administration.

The persistence of tradition rather than policy is compounded by district turnover, which often means that an administrator who *finally* understands the importance of counseling in school improvement is replaced by one who has not yet come to that conclusion. The individual who supervises counselors may have the ear of an important superintendent, but in other cases may not. Just as the system seems to be working, the actors can change:

> A key area superintendent, who reported directly to the [head] superintendent and [Person A], left. Now that was two [key people] who were gone. Then [Person B] left, almost after a year, again because of a lot of turmoil, changes, challenges, fighting, and

politics in the system. Then came [Person C, who] is now the area superintendent. . . . So, you started with [Person A], who then had to report to [Person B] who now has to report to [Person C]. You follow that? So we had to take [Person C] up to Washington and California and let him learn. No sooner than he got back, guess what? They move him and [Person D] is now in his place.

As the resource noose is tightened, district staff members accumulate unfamiliar roles and become fragmented. Rather than hire a new person to replace a departing director of counseling services, one superintendent in our study added the oversight of counseling to the duties of the director of instructional services. The vacuum created by personnel shifts and role overload reinforces the lack of consistent policies and expectations about counselor roles in school improvement. Counselors are overlooked rather than deliberately excluded. A counselor at one site expressed this frustration:

> I feel it's disappointing that we're not involved at the level we could be. We could be, and we want to be, but we're not. . . . As far as being on those school improvement committees, I'm sure we have representation, but are we being used as real active members? I don't think so.

While the absence of district policies and expectations is one problem, other policies undermine more effective use of student support personnel. Site-based management—another key element of school reform in many of the districts—increases pressure on principals to focus exclusively on their building. Superintendents who prefer that principals stay in their building throughout the school day reinforce the use of student support staff as adjunct administrators, since their absence is less noticeable.

Flexible resources are, of course, always a problem for schools because 85% or more of the budget is allocated to relatively inflexible personnel costs. At least five of the seven districts we studied lacked resources to support counselors in data-driven decision making to develop academic programs for students. In some, there were insufficient funds to upgrade counselors' skills to manage the task, while in others the district's student databases were not easily accessible to building-level counselors in a form that was useful. In one district, for example, it was not possible to merge student information systems that contained grades, attendance, standardized test results, and health records—except manually. As an administrator in another district notes, "We have a lot of information that our counselors don't know how to access. . . . It is a great big vat, and you can't pull it out in a form that's usable."

The changing demographics of many school districts also contributes to the need for information at all levels, while at the same time creating competing pressures for more teaching services for students in need of second language support or special education services. Demographic changes are often accompanied by increased student mobility, which creates information gaps as the availability of student records lags behind the movement of students from one building or district to another.

The way in which districts conduct their daily business also affects efforts by student support personnel and school-based administrators to make them part of the reform team. Administrative turnover creates a policy vacuum that deprives student support personnel of a centralized voice in school improvement. Student support gets sucked into the black hole of "other duties as assigned" due to lack of central support or an articulated alternative vision. Districts lack resources, such as simplified databases, to enable student support staff to perform new duties and cannot afford the needed upgrades at a time when they also need to pay for increased testing and accountability requirements. Moreover, changes in education funding formulas force districts to set fiscal priorities that often do not include professional development funds for student support personnel to retrain themselves to adapt to districts' changing demographics, social tensions, or the national focus on achievement and accountability.

LIMITED RESOURCES?
EMPHASIZE COLLABORATION

Before we turn to our observations about systemic improvement, we want to emphasize that even within settings that are not particularly supportive, significant strides toward integrating student support programs into the academic focus of schools can be made with limited resources. The key is usually programmatic, small-scale initiatives that principals and student support staff design to demonstrate how they all can make the teachers' job easier. When teachers see student support staff as true partners, they are often willing to change their own jobs to collaborate. Here are two examples.

Valley Magnet School

Valley Magnet School, with a 7–12 grade configuration, draws students from all over the sprawling district in which it is located. The counselor and the principal articulate a clear image of what is needed: role differentiation among the counseling staff, teamwork with the principal, and interventions that will help teachers.

Part of the head counselor's strategy, negotiated with the principal, was to release counselors from yard duty to team with a teacher to deliver career and college counseling modules to middle school students:

The teacher who was teaching the education career planning was an English teacher. She did a very good job with careers and things, but nothing about college and postsecondary options, so I talked my principal into giving that teaching position to a counselor. . . . [The teacher] has the backside of that class, so the kids take one class one semester, and then the other class. So I have a team [of teacher and counselor] there.

In a state where counselors do not have to be certified teachers, she has encountered little resistance because she has tried to focus on teacher's problems:

They [teachers] would like us to do more, simply because they're convinced that it makes their job easier. If they work with me, I can go into the 8th grade to tell them, "Here are the graduation requirements. You have to do this, this, and this to graduate. Here are some ways to do this, this, and this. The kids work harder if they know what they're working for.

Flatlands Middle School

Flatlands Middle School reorganized the student support team to include a teacher (part time), and a collaborator with the school-based Parent Center. The initial programs resulted in tangible improvements in student behavior and home-school connections. With the strong advocacy of the principal, the faculty voted to eliminate one faculty position in favor of an additional counselor:

See, we're blessed that our faculty also voted for us to have a full-time dean out of the classroom, and the [teacher member of the counseling team] is also funded in full. So, the faculty has really done their part in trying to assist the whole child, you know, because their classes are a whole lot of. . . . It's more work. We're working with kids, and these days, it's tough for teachers and counselors.

In addition, to relieve the burden of constant crisis intervention, the counseling team decided to adopt a "counselor of the day" staffing policy. One of the four counselors does full-time duty in the front office, dealing with discipline, parent concerns, inquiries from social service agencies, and so forth. This position rotates, so that the counselors who are "off" have a regular schedule to work with teachers, the Parent Center, student groups, and others. The counselors believe that this has enhanced their ability to prove to teachers that they are an integral part of the student achievement picture.

CONCLUSION

School and district administrators need to consider the barriers and assets unique to each school to significantly change an existing student support structure. We have considered the following factors in this chapter:

1. **District and School Characteristics.** The uniqueness of each school at different levels constitutes a barrier. As we noted in Chapter 2 and again in this chapter, student support roles are configured differently from school to school, so no single structural solution will achieve new models for all student support programs.

2. **District and School Champions of Organizational Change.** Schools and districts that are moving toward new models of student support have found champions of change in a wide variety of places. In some, a respected counselor's advocacy is, with district support, enough to move a system. In others, the most visible movers and shakers are principals. Changing the system means finding the energy and the advocacy, irrespective of formal position.

3. **District and School-Level Actors Engaged in Organizational Change.** It is good to have everyone on board, but, in most districts, this is unrealistic. Changing student support structures means creating clusters of active participants throughout the system rather than waiting for a single vision to emerge.

4. **Standard Operating Procedures (Both Structural and Cultural) That Impede or Facilitate Organizational Change.** Will site-based management keep principals or student support staff from leaving their buildings to work as a team? Will the lack of a district-level job description for student support professionals prevent consensus about a direction for new student support? What policies can be changed and what must be worked around?

5. **Competing or Complementary Reform Agendas.** Every district has multiple reforms, some of which compete for time and resources with student support, and some of which may complement reformed student support. For example, understanding how a comprehensive support program can complement a district priority on teaching reading at the secondary level may be critical to creating backing for change.

6. **Resource Reallocations to Support the Change Effort.** Many times, a district or school will signal its support for a reform initiative by reallocating resources. Under current fiscal constraints, it is reasonable to assume that new resources to significantly change

the scope and focus of student support programs will be limited, particularly at the district level. District personnel must collaborate with schools to figure out how to reallocate the human resources that already exist, as in case of Flatlands Middle School, where a teacher was assigned part time to the student support team.

We don't want to make it sound as if the student support system in all or even most schools is broken. Our perspective concerns the *underutilization* of human resources in improving schools, particularly those focused on students who are, for one reason or another, likely to perform below their potential. Good intentions and goals for increased achievement are not enough. In spite of the best efforts of collaborators from districts, schools, and universities, only two of the seven districts that we studied made major strides in a systemic reorganization of the role of counselors, making them part of the reform agenda. And, even in those districts, implementation at the school level was spotty. As we move forward, we need to recognize that progress must be made on a school-by-school basis, because even when districts or states are more active in setting and monitoring school goals, we know that principals are the main force determining how effectively professionals collaborate within schools.

All seven districts that we studied were involved with externally funded programs to change the role of counselors, but the presence of additional or temporary resources does not guarantee success at either the district or school level. In the next chapter, we will look at more systemic reforms that were possible when two districts used external grants as a lever for initiating change.

New Practices Defined

4

In this chapter you will

- Look at two schools that have reorganized to become more effective.
- Learn what is involved in new-vision support.
- See a portrait of a student support staff in action being leaders, advocates, and data-based decision makers.

SCHOOL REORGANIZATION

Implementing reformed practices first requires an image of what is involved. In this chapter, we provide descriptions of principals who have restructured their organizational systems to include student support staff in significant leadership positions within the school. The magnitude of role shift required to move student support personnel from sitting on the sidelines to being proactive advocates and leaders in promoting the academic achievement of all students is apparent when we look at it in terms of the four key functions outlined in Chapter 2: academic advising, career counseling, personal/social support, and community engagement.

The following examples should help you visualize how a reformed, comprehensive student support program might look in your school. With each example and suggestion, you must ask yourself how such a change would work in your school, with its unique staff, collection of problems, and potential.

IMAGES OF REORGANIZED
STUDENT SUPPORT PROGRAMS

Student support programs can be reorganized and redesigned to focus on learning and ensuring student academic success, but no models currently exist for principals to use in restructuring their human resource staff functions. Although the stimulus for change may vary in response to local conditions and initiatives, the goal of meeting academic, career, and personal/social agendas is the same. The following examples illustrate different organizational restructuring patterns in two schools that began incorporating student support personnel into successful teams to practice this new vision of support.

Wellington Middle School: Restructuring Into Student Support Teams

Wellington Middle School has grown rapidly in the last few years to reach an enrollment of 750 students. Some 81% of these students receive free or reduced lunch and about the same percentage are children of color, primarily Hmong. In the past, the school had problems with high truancy rates, low test scores, and a culture filled with disciplinary problems. Now, with the restructuring of the support staff, the school prides itself on its increased attendance rate as well as its discipline and academic referral system, which keeps kids on track to learn.

Principal Stuart Long designated improving the school's poor attendance rate as his first priority. "You can't get students to learn if they don't show up." Principal Long made two structural changes to this end, an example of blending reforms, discussed in Chapter 3. In this case, the support system staff was overhauled simultaneously with and as part of restructuring the school's homeroom system, which had been primarily individual teachers supervising silent reading.

The school reorganized from a top-down management approach to a team model, as the old homerooms were replaced by an advisory system geared toward increasing attendance and student progress. Part of Principal Long's vision required adding more student support personnel to the staff. An attendance team was created, consisting of two administrators, two social workers, two counselors, a counseling assistant, three attendance educational assistants, and two teachers.

Principal Long made it clear that the new system had been put in place to codify attendance, discipline, and academic progress, and that all staff were accountable for results. This illustrates the point made in the previous chapter that "changing structures rarely accomplishes a great deal without accompanying changes in people's assumptions and behavior." The new system of attendance interventions, represented in Figure 4.1, helps to create accountability. As Principal Long says,

> I'm a systems data kind of person. . . . That's because, if you're talking about accountability, and you're talking about where a teacher fits into something, if I don't tell you what my expectations are of you, how can I hold you accountable to that?

Figure 4.1   Attendance Interventions

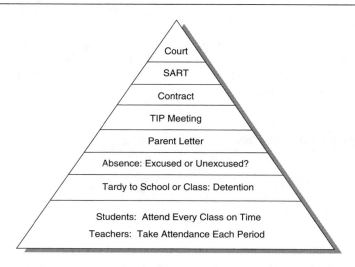

SOURCE: Pyramid figures in Chapter 4 are used with permission of Washington Technology Magnet Middle School, Saint Paul, MN.

NOTES: Explanation of terms: TIP = Truancy Intervention Program; Contract = Parents and students are invited to the school to sign a contract with an assistant principal and advocate; SART = Student Assistance Review Team, which meets with parents and students, reviews documents, and develops a plan to increase student attendance.

The attendance team implemented a pyramid model like the one outlined in Chapter 2—with academics on one side, behavior on the other, and attendance as the base. The formula created by the team was that academics + good behavior + attendance = SUCCESS. In order to keep track of attendance, the team came up with the referral system in Figure 4.2.

Figure 4.2   Discipline Interventions

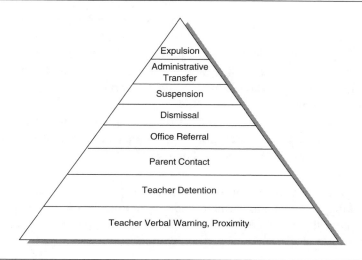

Teachers are in charge of attendance and are responsible every day for alerting the rest of the team when a student is tardy or absent. Each support staff member is in charge of a specific level within the pyramid of discipline interventions so that no student falls off the radar screen. The system has been judged a success, because the daily attendance rate has increased to 93%!

In addition to attendance, the team has created a similar system for discipline as well as for academic referrals. According to the principal, "You start with what happens in the classroom. Teachers have the proximity. Then, we have a system where the teachers can give the student detention, and move up to where the parent gets contacted, then an office referral, and so forth."

The school's academic team is composed of counselors, a nurse, administrators, a special education representative, and two social workers. A student who is failing two or more core classes is referred to a counselor by the homeroom teacher, and the counselor in turn brings these referrals to the academic team. The attendance team meets with the academic team to discuss the referrals and information is communicated back to the homeroom teacher so everyone remains in the loop. The school's system of academic interventions is represented in Figure 4.3.

Principal Stuart Long sees his support staff as an essential component to his system of success.

Figure 4.3 Academic Interventions

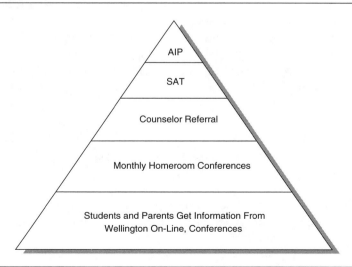

NOTES: Explanation of terms: SAT = Student Assistance Team, composed of counselors, social workers, administrators, a nurse, and teachers; AIP = Academic Intervention Program. The counselor brings the at-risk student's name to the SAT committee. If there are not extenuating circumstances, the student is removed from an elective class and assigned to an AIP for one period to make up missing work and develop study skills.

Mountainview High School: A New Way of Organizing and Supporting Student Needs

Peter Sans is the principal of a high school with a population of 1,266 students, 77% of whom are minorities and 78% of whom are eligible for free and reduced lunch. The school has been heavily impacted by an incoming immigrant population—anywhere from 700 to 750 of the students entering the school did not pass the state tests due to language or other barriers. This change in demographics in the recent years has led Principal Sans to refocus the goal of school from a programmatic model to one with a more cultural and student-centered focus. In order to do this, Principal Sans first restructured his school into small learning communities well before the district had decided to move in that direction.

He also decided that, due to the size of the immigrant population, cultural competence and sensitivity would be a priority for all students. When certain staff retired, Principal Sans decided to hire both a Spanish- and Hmong-speaking family liaison to work full-time with all of the staff.

One common barrier to school reform today, mentioned in Chapter 3, is the lack of new resources to meet increased expectations. Principal Sans did what every change master needs to do in this situation—increase the flexibility of existing staff. As Principal Sans stated,

> So, we had to be more flexible, we had to be more student centered. I had to communicate to staff that, whatever decisions were going to be made, were going to be made in the best interests of kids and, given the benefit of the doubt, it would go towards the support of students. The parents had to be more actively involved, and if they weren't, then we had to reach out and create that kind of activity. There wasn't going to be top-down decision making; we were all going to be part of the decision, but ultimately it had to be to the betterment of students, not of staffing, and not of seniority.

In order to save resources, Principal Sans hired Educational Assistants to do much of the time-consuming paperwork and clerical work previously assigned to counselors.

In addition, while keeping the budget the same, the principal made it a priority when staff in the building retired, to hire new staff with the same philosophy as his. When getting ready to hire a new counselor, he told prospective candidates,

> What I tell anybody who interviews, if you are coming just to be a counselor, if you are coming just to be a teacher, then this isn't the place, because we got to be more than that. So, our counselors

will do home visits, our counselors will interact with agencies, our counselors will interact with parents. Our counselors work with kids. But they understand that kids are a priority—that paperwork is not, that a student's dignity is not something that we will put in peril.

After the initial restructuring, Principal Sans continued to push all staff to become student centered by having them focus on three areas: rigor, personalization, and accountability. By highlighting those three concepts, by being flexible, but also by being clear about what the school needs to do as far as instruction, interpersonal dynamics with kids and the families, and how they work with each other as a team, he has been able to maintain the school's course of direction.

Principal Sans counts his student support staff among the top members of his school team. With two social workers, three counselors, two community-family liaisons, two attendants, a group of supporting attendants, and a full-time school psychologist, it is clear that he is a firm believer in having a solid student support team. Unlike most principals, Peter Sans spent 16 years as a counselor, so he was better able to appreciate the potential of his student support staff than most.

It is extremely important to Principal Sans that all the support staff communicate with each other on a weekly basis to discuss identified students so that there is no overlapping. All staff must be aware of who is working with specific students and must maintain the connectedness of the team.

In addition to communicating with each other, the support staff participated with the 9th and 10th grade teams, so they could follow students' instruction and academic progress.

Principal Sans restructured his school to be more student centered and demonstrated the importance of being a distributive leader in the process. The result is that staff and students get better access to student support, and feel more connected to their school. As a consequence, attendance has increased and test scores are going up. Principal Sans believes that his change from being a top-down leader to a student-centered leader was the catalyst for changing the whole school culture and system. In fact, he sees himself as a support person in his school:

I often tell staff that I am a support person in the building. And I see myself as a support person. And [I tell staff] that it is really important for me to support anyone from the custodians to the people in the cafeteria to the classroom teacher to the social worker, that I am here to support them and [do] what I can relative to resources to whatever kind of support. . . . If I am able to walk the walk and talk the talk, so to speak, then I think it is easier for everybody else to accept that kind of concept. [The staff] has to see me as a support person in order to come to me for support. So, I have to exemplify. So, I have to model what I expect of them. I don't always have to be the decision maker— in most cases I am not—but I have to let people know and I have to give them, help them, develop the confidence to make those decisions, and if it doesn't work, it is not that they failed; it is just that it didn't work—a "let's try something else" kind of mentality.

What Is Involved in New-Vision Programs?

According to Keys and Lockhart, "A multi-systemic perspective suggests that in order to understand a student's behavior, [student support personnel] need to be familiar with the multiple, interrelated systems that are an ongoing part of a student's life."[1] This means that students are embedded in the wide variety of societal challenges that we introduced in Chapter 1. By analyzing the multiple, overlapping, and incompatible expectations of the different worlds that students inhabit (but over which they have little control), we can better understand what they need in order to navigate their way through school.

Systems theory begins with the individual, but involves not only psychological development, but also the environment that affects each person's relationships and interactions. Systems theory also assumes that a change in one area of a system affects all other areas and, in effect, changes the system. We draw a distinction between student support programs that are individually focused and those that are systems focused. We argue that, unlike individual approaches, "A systems paradigm views causality as interactive and circular."[2] In other words, you can't change any one part without other issues arising.

Student support personnel, therefore, must use multiple approaches and understand system dynamics in order to help a child succeed in school. Among their most important jobs is helping teachers work with children who are pushed and pulled by multiple, overlapping, and incompatible expectations. To give a simple example, Principal Jack Partir, in Chapter 3, noted that many impoverished middle school students who come to school out of uniform are not defiant, but, rather, don't have an adult who is able to provide them with clean clothing. Punishing the child does not solve the problem.

Real support for your vision means restructuring all regular points of contact that your student support staff have with students, teachers, and administrators in order to break the inertia of the old system. In general, the academic achievement of economically disadvantaged students and students of color illustrates a systemic disparity, and their improvement must serve as a yardstick to measure the success or failure of a reform initiative.[3] Verbal and emotional support alone would not have sustained the transformations we have described at Wellington or Mountainview schools: The key tools for change were new role definitions and new benchmarks for performance.

TAKING ON LEADERSHIP FOR INCREASED STUDENT ACHIEVEMENT

House and Hayes contend that counselors—and, again, we add all student support staff—must take a proactive leadership role in their schools and advocate for the success of all students.[4] As in the case of Principal Peter Sans, any principal involved in distributive leadership must give away certain decision-making authority by creating and encouraging other leaders in the school. As we argued in previous chapters, student support personnel are in a unique position to fill these emerging leadership roles, because they are available and trained to work in all four functional areas: academic advising, career counseling, personal/social support, and community engagement. But what does "leadership" from the student support staff perspective mean, in practice? And how can principals promote such leadership?

Truman High School provides an example of a counseling department initiating change in their school in order to increase student achievement.

Truman High School

Truman High School is a 2,700-student school that has shown consistent improvement on state achievement tests over the past few years. Located in a mixed income area near Los Angeles, the school is predominantly white and lower-middle-class, but 30% of its students are nonnative English speakers, and 48%—well above the state average—are eligible for subsidized lunch. The school prides itself, in particular, on its student retention and its strong academic programs, which try to ensure that all students are prepared for postsecondary education.

This success is no accident. After a traumatic incident several years ago in which a student was assaulted outside of the school, the head of the counseling department decided that things needed to be done differently. With license from the principal, counselors reorganized the student support program into specialty domains with specific counselors assigned to each area. Two counselors took on academic support, which involved all the programming of students, the master schedule, and getting students into the right courses to ensure that they were on track for graduation and postsecondary work. Although many counselors detest scheduling, the two who volunteered were excited about improving a job that usually results in weeks of headaches and complaints for the whole staff. As one person noted, "It's a lot of administrative work, but if you have an organizational head, and you can figure out a system, you can make change that will make a difference."

Another counselor, who had dual training in school counseling and family therapy, took responsibility for personal and social counseling. A third domain was career counseling, which involved working with first-year students and sophomores, and also dealt with most of the testing associated with career guidance. The final staff person was the college counselor.

Recognizing that fires will always exist in high schools, the team decided to have a Counselor of the Day, with each of the five counselors taking one day a week. This freed the other four from disciplinary problems, walk-in conferences with parents, and the other routine business of managing student services.

The result? Counselors believe that they have more time to pursue their passion and to provide better services to larger numbers of students. The head of student support, whose domain was college counseling, notes,

> Oh, we do the programming a little differently. We're going into classrooms. We have our manuals. Every student has a program. I can call up a classroom of kids like that [snaps his fingers] and know where they are academically. We go into all the English classes, at least once or twice a semester. We tell them, "This is what you're going to need. If you want to go to [a University of California school], this is what you've got to do. If you want to go to [a California State University school], this is what you've got to do. And if you've been failing, you're going to need to take summer school." . . . So a lot of information is going on, a lot of exchange, because they're doing classrooms instead of [doing] one-on-one [counseling].

Similarly, the personal-social counselor said,

> Oh, yeah, you know, I do a lot of crises and emergencies, but we all handle that. But I'm [primarily working with] groups of kids. I've got kids at risk, I've got divorced kids, I've a group for this, a group for that. And I go into classrooms. When the teacher has a topic on something related to mental health, getting along, conflict management, I go in and do a lesson, so the kids get it. Isn't this a wonderful model for high school? Career counselor, college counselor—same thing. . . . [We're] out in classrooms, talking to kids, with an organized program.

An individual outside of the student support office observed that counselors were ecstatic about their increased professionalism, which allowed them to know when they could say "no" to a request from the principal. One of the counselors noted, "You know, the principal wanted to make sure that I was watching all the kids, doing lunchroom duty, and all that." She picks up her binoculars and says, "This is how I do it. I look out the window there. Yep, I see them. I don't do lunchroom duty."

Overall, the counselors thought that, aside from providing better services to students, they were also more accountable than they were when their caseload consisted of "all students with the last names E–K." One of the academic-scheduling counselors observed, "if 70% of the seniors are having trouble graduating, they know who is responsible. If we have a huge problem with depression, they know that . . . the personal-social counselor needs to take more responsibility."

As a leader in the school, a new-vision support team like the one in Truman High School might provide data snapshots of student outcomes, show implications of those data, point out achievement gaps for particular subpopulations of students, and provide leadership for the school community to work toward equity for all students. Actions taken by the student support teams to address identified achievement gaps might focus on planning and implementing prevention programs, career/college activities, course selection and placement activities, and initiatives with teachers that focus on strengthening the social/personal behaviors of students in the classroom and school.

School counselors and other support personnel can play critical leadership roles in schools, but it's the principal's responsibility to promote proactive leadership and teamwork among his or her staff. A practicing school counselor describes her school's leadership team below:

In my school, I'm part of what they call a *Leadership Team*. We meet every Wednesday morning at 7:15, and everything that happens at school happens through the Leadership Team pretty much. All the information is put out in the team, and then it goes out to the rest of the faculty, and anything that's happening, your team usually knows first. It's part of what [our district] calls "the design for education," and that's part of it—having the leadership team collaboratively coming up with good solutions to help better the school, instead of one person being the "This is the way it is, and this is the way it's going to become." A lot of things are done on a team kind of mentality.

This statement is also reflective of the mentality of Principal Peter Sans. What would you as an *administrative leader* have to do in order to reorganize your school into *leadership teams* that are effective at creating positive change? The resources in Chapters 5 and 6 provide guidelines on how to create these teams and how you can develop into a more effective, distributive leader.

Distributed leadership can take various forms. For student support staff, it may mean taking on an issue within the school that has been designated by the principal and making important decisions in order to improve success rates. For example, this counselor talks about taking a leadership role to help increase attendance rates in her school:

> I have been involved with our school's continuous improvement plan in terms of working with a group of students with attendance problems—students who are not quite truant, but who do not come to school on a consistent basis. As a result, we have seen an improvement in our schoolwide attendance rate.

In another school, the main function of a counselor in a leadership role might be focusing on mediation and conflict resolution to improve the school climate and encourage student achievement:

> I've been involved in a schoolwide effort to reduce the amount of conflict, whether it is fighting or just disruptions in the classroom. This focus on conflict resolution is reflected in the types of small groups that I offered this year. I was able to offer a series of groups for Grades K through 5. Teachers identified children they were concerned about. As we revise our home guidance program in the district, we are trying to focus on helping children succeed academically by reducing barriers to academic success at home.

As a change master, the principal's role is to identify, create, and encourage leaders and leadership roles in the school, and then to provide the resources and authority to proceed.

STUDENT SUPPORT PROFESSIONALS AS ADVOCATES AND DATA-BASED DECISION MAKERS

As a principal, it is important for you to recognize your student support team members as advocates, which requires the empowerment inherent in distributive leadership. In new-vision student support programs, distributive leadership and advocacy are different sides of the same coin. An advocate is someone who works on behalf of another person. In the same way, the definition of an advocate can be broadened to include someone who works on behalf of the whole system.

As in distributive leadership, the change master is concerned with the whole school organization and distributes school leadership functions to the staff, empowering them to make critical decisions that affect school processes. All members of the school should be reorganized, so that they work collaboratively as advocates for teachers' and students' needs in all four function areas: academic advising, career counseling, personal/ social support, and community engagement. The idea of the student support staff as advocates in no way undermines the role of the teacher as an advocate; their roles as advocates are cooperative and complementary, not competitive. All staff members have student interests at heart; it is the job of the principal to find the best ways of reorganizing the school to maximize the effectiveness of their efforts.

As advocates for the achievement of all students, new-vision student support staff persons might alter their traditional roles in a variety of ways. By using data analysis skills, they can help the whole school community to look at student outcomes beyond a particular classroom setting. Data can also be used to effect change by demonstrating the need to call on resources from both school and community. In organizing student needs using criteria more relevant than the first initial of last name, they can provide experiences that will broaden students' career and college awareness. What these advocacy roles have in common is a focus on the whole student in the context of the school, the community, and the world.

The use of data to target specific populations of students need not be restricted to college and career. Student support personnel can identify students by risk factors, interests, or abilities to develop appropriate interventions or mechanisms for advancement. The following case is an example that complements some of the exercise work done in Chapter 2.

Adelman High School: New Counselors in Action—At-Risk Student Intervention

The principal at Adelman High School, an urban school, is a mover and a shaker. She wants things to be happening, and for all key players in the school to get on board.

The principal and the student support staff agreed that this year should be devoted to the at-risk student population. Adelman counselors, with the help of the principal, initiated a specific intervention called Our Kids, which used early screening and background information to predict who in the incoming 9th grade class might be most likely to drop out of school before graduating. The counselors and administrators actively recognized that these indicators may have easily been missed in the past and interventions delayed until a crisis occurred.

The Our Kids program outlined some initial criteria to identify those most at risk. Once students were identified, they were assigned a counselor to address the difficulties encountered during the school year in order to keep them educationally on track. All guidance staff identified the barriers to success for these students and what steps could be taken to remove them, including small academic-skills training groups. In this way, at-risk students were connected to a specific counselor before problems occurred.

The Process

After researching at-risk student interventions, the Adelman support team developed specific eligibility criteria and created a one-on-one intake interview for each at-risk student. After selecting the eligible students, the guidance team began the intervention process. The process started with an intake questionnaire in order to provide baseline data. The result of the questionnaire provided pertinent information for the support team to set up interventions throughout the school year.

At the beginning of the school year, the students who were identified through Our Kids were directed through counselor referrals to in-school resources, such as the school social worker, for serious personal and family problems, or the Truancy Intervention Program (TIP). There was also a set of interventions developed to support and help these students in school. The interventions were as follows:

- **Ongoing Academic Assessment.** Along with the referral given by the counselors, there were quite a few interventions provided by the student support team. One of the most important was the ongoing monitoring and assessment of student progress throughout the year. With the monitoring, the students were able to get rapid feedback on their progress along with frequent positive reinforcement for staying on track.

- **Presentation of School Requirements.** At the beginning of the year, the students participated in a directed presentation, which was provided to clarify and specify all of the needed requirements for graduation. This provided an early understanding of the things the students had to achieve during the year.

- **Small Group Counseling.** Small groups of approximately 12 to 13 people were developed to foster open discussions about academic improvement and relationship building within the school. This helped create a connection to the school for many of the students. The students were directed to stay abreast of their own personal progress in school by documenting their academic achievement and involvement in school activities via a planning Web site. This type of approach has been effective in reinforcing personal responsibility for schoolwork while also facilitating a secure environment to discuss academically related topics.

- **Communication of Results to Staff.** The principal insisted that this type of intervention initiative is incomplete without direct, two-way communication among the support team, the teachers, and the rest of the school's staff. The support team specifically made the effort to ask the staff what they thought might be missing, what might be done to improve the process, and where they might go in the future. As a result, there were very positive responses from the teachers, and many inquired as to how they could be more involved.

An important aspect of this vignette is that student support personnel are advocates not only for students, but for teachers as well. Communication and team building between teachers and student support personnel increase the effectiveness of all staff functions. When teachers and support staff are on the same team, they are able to work together to improve instruction and assessment. In one school that we researched, the student support staff and teachers worked together to create a curriculum for a new advisory program in the school. Both groups took equal responsibility for implementation of and adjustments to the new curriculum. In addition, the student support staff cotaught some of the lessons in classrooms, further blurring the once rigid lines separating student support staff from teachers.

The Our Kids program at Adelman demonstrates how crucial data-based decision making is in proactive leadership. Without the use of data to identify potential problems, staff are reduced to reacting after problems occur. Many principals have undergone training for data-based decision making, but, as a principal, it is impossible to do this alone. In fact, student support personnel are the only people on your staff in a position to implement systematic data-based decision making in an organized manner throughout your school.

The scope of work for a new-vision student support program stresses that student support staff must be competent users of data and technology. Your support staff should be able to use data to assess and interpret needs; recognize differences in culture, languages, values, and backgrounds; establish and assess measurable goals for student outcomes; assess barriers in the building that impede learning or academic success; and interpret student data for use by the whole school in planning for change. The following example is one way you, as a principal, can utilize your support staff for data gathering and analyzing.

Data-Based Decision Making: Assessing the Needs of Students and Teachers

Counselors at one large, urban high school attended a data-based decision-making workshop. Since then, they have found innovative ways to gather and share information with teachers and staff. For example, in the spring, counselors gathered information, via a quick e-mail survey, about the kinds of career activities teachers do with students. After putting the results of the questionnaire into a database, the counselors used the information to tailor their own career counseling activities.

This year, the counselors have compiled a database of SAT10 scores of 9th graders to give to teachers. With this database in hand, they used a faculty/staff meeting to explain how to interpret the scores and use them in decision making.

Another way counselors used their data-based decision-making skills was to give all 9th grade students a learning style inventory in order to share the information with both the students and their teachers.

> The counselors in this school believe it is important to share the results of surveys and tests with students and teachers. At another meeting, they explained how to interpret ACT scores, highlighting the strengths and weaknesses of their own students' scores and providing breakdowns by racial and ethnic groups. These scores were then put in context by explaining their local colleges' and universities' ACT requirements. This gave teachers the information they needed to focus instruction on areas that needed further work.

Creating Student Support and Teacher Teams

As a principal, it is important to recognize the importance of communication and collaboration between all members of your school. Remember that a new-vision school support person does not work in isolation. Rather, with your impetus, student support professionals should regularly consult with teams of teachers, administrators, and other educators for problem solving and information sharing. These student support and teacher teams are designed to identify and address whole-school and whole-system concerns with your guidance, thus ensuring responsiveness to all areas of your school that need special attention. For example, teams can be created around equity and diversity issues, working within the school or with groups or agencies in the community.

Always driven by the data, there are endless possibilities for teachers and student support staff to team to address incentives or remove barriers to student achievement. You, the change master, shape the process and mechanisms by which leaders are allowed to develop and exercise real authority. Both student support staff and teachers become equally dedicated to developing staff training and team responses to students' academic, social, emotional, and developmental needs.

As one counselor points out, this collaboration with teachers and others in the school is an essential part of new-vision support:

> A lot of it goes back to collaboration; they taught us to look at ourselves, not just the counseling department ourselves, but to be the leader of the counseling program, and then collaborate with the other people in the schools, with business partners, with teachers, and have them do as much of the counseling program as you can. You're kind of the leader of those initiatives.

In addition to student support and teacher teams, principals must recognize the importance of a comprehensive support program in which school counselors collaborate with school psychologists, paraprofessionals, nurses, and social workers. As we mentioned earlier, these roles have also evolved as quasi-independent appendices to the school's structure, which leads to a silo kind of thinking. In such a silo system, students tend to be assessed by the nature of a dominant issue and then assigned to the professional responsible for that issue. The problem with this mentality is that most students' needs are complex and overlap into other domains. The only way to advocate for the whole child is to foster regular communication between teams and to put a mix of professionals together on the same team.

Only you, as a principal and change master, can facilitate the change in thinking from a series of compartmentalized service-delivery methods to a comprehensive support program with child advocacy at the center. Chapters 5 and 6 will provide practical guidelines for this transition.

Mental Health, Revisited

Many schools, especially those with high populations of poverty, have problems that need to be dealt with on a social and mental-health level. The case of Jack Partir, in Chapter 3, demonstrates how difficult it is to keep kids with extreme social or mental-health issues on a productive learning track. We believe that social, personal, and mental-health issues must be dealt with on a regular basis, but we do not think that one-on-one counseling or therapy is the best way to utilize your student support personnel. Although new-vision student support professionals do employ counseling with students, groups, and families, they do so in coordination with a wide variety of services within the school and drawn from the community.

Mental Health Issues:
The Importance of Community Resources

Principal Sans believes it is important for his school to work with community agencies that come into the building on a regular basis:

> Everything from single-parent group meetings, we have the YMCA coming in, we have African American male groups, we have Latina groups. So, just about anything that a kid has outside of school, we bring it here to school, and it is really important for me as a building principal to maintain that connectiveness from community to here . . . hence our support staff. So, I tell them that they can't be everything to everybody, but they can refer or they can connect kids and families, and it doesn't make sense for a family to be working with a community agency outside of school. It helps us and I think it makes kids and families feel more comfortable if they see those people in our school.

With the breakdown of the walls that separate the functions of student support professionals, personal and social issues are dealt with through a system where the student support member acts as an advocate for students to get the help they need to stay on track to learn.

CONCLUSION

We believe that creating a comprehensive support program is the best way for all student support professionals to communicate and coordinate the four function areas of academic advising, career counseling, personal/social support, and community engagement. As we mentioned earlier, we visualize the CSP as a team model, one that includes mechanisms and time built into the system for regular meetings and for frequent triage so that all of the parts work in a cohesive way to increase student health and achievement. A new vision will not be realized until it is formulated into actions that are communicated and established by the principal.

Visualizing images of what your reformed student support program will look like is an important first step in beginning the process of change. We have tried to provide you with images to begin this process. In some of our cases, the school principal centralized the student support office, which made communicating as a team easier. The result in the cases of Principals Peter Sans and Stuart Long was that communication between student support staff increased, which made the student support functions run more smoothly without overlap. In addition, coordination between support staff and administrators was more streamlined, with regular communication processes within the schools.

You must decide if centralization and integration are workable in your school. We do know that, in some cases, having a central office location that houses all student support personnel may not be feasible or worth the effort. Our intention is to help you, as a principal, visualize and understand the importance of integrating student support programs—via a central office or other form of integration—so that all functions are addressed and all students benefit from the system. If a central student support office is not an option in your school, there are many other ways to limit the development of silos and strict role differentiation among staff. Some of these ideas are outlined in the next two chapters.

In the Beginning   **5**

What School Leaders
Can Do About Student Support

In this chapter you will

- Begin to apply what you have learned about new models of student support to your school.
- Learn about some tools that will help you define and analyze your current situation and plan for change.
- Discuss some of the strategies that will help to address the four preconditions for change: clarity and relevance, action images, will, and skill.

To the troops on the ground, the succession of plans and programs working their way through the American education system often appears like this:

All school staff members are assembled in the cafeteria, where the principal hands out an announcement of a district grant from a larger foundation that will provide support for improving instruction in all schools. The focus of the grant is on increasing student achievement and closing the gap between high- and lower-income students. In the past few years, other programs, including teacher career ladders, pay-for-performance programs, new national math and science curricula, and total quality management have been touted as meeting the same need. This one, says the principal, is different—there will be resources, including professional development provided by national consultants, and some release time for a teacher to help monitor implementation. It's The New Thing, and the principal bravely discusses the virtues and the benefits to a tired staff, who have a cup of coffee and eat one of the day-old donuts, and head for their cars muttering, "Here we go again—it's the reform du jour."

If this scenario sounds familiar, you know that you will have to do something different if you are to take advantage of what we have defined as the 10% solution—integrating your student support resources with academic achievement in your school. The previous chapters offered a number of images and ideas about what needs to be done to accomplish this; the current chapter takes the next step, focusing on the role of school leaders in creating readiness for change.

APPROACHES TO CHANGE

We assume that you accept your role as a change master, but you may not know exactly how to proceed. This chapter is built around the basic steps outlined in Chapter 1: removing barriers and working on preconditions. In the next chapter, we will address some of the issues that arise in early implementation, including adapting and adjusting, while using distributed leadership to your advantage.

A Unique Challenge

In the final two chapters of this book, we emphasize specifics about integrating student support personnel into the school's student learning and development agenda. *This specificity is important, because you are faced with a particularly challenging task. The images presented in Chapter 2 are bare bones, and there are no tested, research-based student support models that you can borrow off the shelf.* If you accept that you have untapped human potential you must still begin with an intensive period of design that takes into account the unique features of your school. Consider how the small successes we have found and reported here can be adapted to your school—but be prepared for more midcourse adjustments than may be the case with a more well-developed initiative. And this effort will need to come largely from within your school: You won't find a raft of expert consultants to help you think the issues through, because neither the educational administration nor the school counseling professions have grappled extensively with these issues.

If you are like most school administrators, you must do all of this with a school staff that is often tired and angry with the increasing pressures from accountability initiatives and already overloaded with ideas about what needs to change. But what is the alternative? No change means continuing to waste resources at a time when practicing "random acts of kindness" will not suffice to increase your school's performance.

The educational change literature often assumes either that you are implementing a specific program (such as reading across the curriculum) or a whole-school reform (breaking a large comprehensive high school into smaller learning communities with unique identities and curricula). Working with a change that has the *potential* for affecting the entire school, but which will immediately be most *deeply felt* in one part of the school, poses some unique challenges for principals that will be addressed in the sections of this chapter.

Stimulating Commitment

Your first challenge is to create a sense of excitement within your school about the possibility of change. If the student support professionals are not inspired to be advocates and leaders, and if teachers and administrators do not welcome them as allies, your vision will be marginalized. You need a vanguard group that is willing to experiment and try out new ideas in support of student learning. If at least a few of the counselors, social workers, and others aren't with you, you might feel like throwing in the towel.

Start by considering the personalities and potential of your student support staff. Who will be the foot draggers and who will need some extra motivation? Perhaps you have a "live wire" who has already drawn your attention to ideas that are compatible with your vision. On the other hand, a student development staff that is alternately overworked and complacent about the effectiveness of their performance won't change without some stimulation. And that stimulation will have to come from you, because districts and states rarely pay attention to student support until a crisis occurs, and then that attention is fleeting and not focused on academic achievement.

The Challenge of Creating Visibility

You are central to this change for another reason as well. Counselors and their student support colleagues have been so marginalized by the school reform movement that their role is seldom considered by the average teacher. While ASCA urges their members to be leaders for school change, it is hard to be a leader when your role is overlooked by teachers and administrators. The school principal's visible support is needed in order for counselors and others to have an impact, even if they are ready to spread their wings and fly. Grant High School is a case in point.

Invested Counselors, Absent Principal

Grant High is a small urban school where more than three-quarters of the students are classified as impoverished or minority. During 2003–2004, as the school began phasing in small learning communities, the counselors began planning for a reorganization that would align their work with the new small learning communities (SLC) model. Their program philosophy stressed guidance leadership, data analysis, advocacy, and a direct linkage between professional support staff and student achievement.

Because of the new reform, the counseling department was determined that their offices would have a new look and began a clean-up campaign. If they were going to be doing things differently, they would have to look different. Furthermore, each of the counselors participated on two schoolwide committees, including the Site Council, the School Continuous Improvement Plan (SCIP) Committee, the Attendance Committee, and the Advisory Steering Committee, in order to show their leadership and the integral part they can play in overall school reform.

In spite of their enthusiasm, the counselors found their principal was unsupportive of efforts to implement the new program. One of the main problems was that the idea of the counselors as part of a leadership team did not fit with the principal's mental model of how his school should be run. The principal at Grant believed that the school support staff was ancillary to the school's mission and to the desperate need to reduce the achievement gaps that would place the school on the district and state watch lists. Even though the counselors served on the Advisory Steering Committee, the principal was a consistent no-show at the meetings that they called to discuss the school's new advisory curriculum. The principal was not the only administrator to see other activities as a higher priority; in fact, the administrative team in general did not respond to the counselors' requests for meetings. Consequently, the counselors went about working on the new program and serving on committees without knowing exactly what the principal or other administrators expected.

You don't need to be as insensitive to the opportunities presented by a reformed student support program as the principal of Grant High School to stymie change from below. The support staff in that case had the necessary motivation, but the expectations of teachers did not change. Once you have a handle on your school's *level* of motivation to change, it is time to consider the other half of the equation: How can you *increase* motivation?

UNDERSTANDING BARRIERS

In Chapter 3, we described a set of generic hindrances to more effective student support that we have observed in dozens of secondary schools over the last few years. We hope that this list, based on our research, strikes a chord as you look at your own school. However, we know that no two schools are alike and that each principal must make the issues facing his or her school more concrete if action is to be taken.

As we noted in Chapter 1, most of the current writing on change management pays limited attention to two activities that research on both the individual and small group change processes considers critical: analyzing the forces pressing for and against change, and working to remove barriers. In our view, this omission accounts for the surprisingly low levels of persistence of innovations in U.S. schools and for the prevailing attitude among many educators toward reform—the "and this too shall pass" feeling that the scenario at the beginning of this chapter captured.

When innovation efforts fail, it is common for the principal to feel like a personal failure. After all, if you have put forth a vision for change and the teachers aren't buying it, doesn't that mean that you have failed as a transformational leader—that you lack the charisma and forceful personality to get your message across? You may get discouraged and figure that little can be done until the external pressures become too great, or until the worst naysayer retires.

In the case of renewing your student support system, the biggest problem that you are likely to face is apathy. Your student support staff members are satisfied, and they are used to the way things are, even if they have their complaints. Teachers are unlikely to press for change; most teachers are unaware of the student support professional's work and, without glaring evidence to the contrary, are likely to assume that all is well. Many students and parents simply don't expect much from the student support office until there is a problem. And a big issue may be you: If no one is pressing for change, you might as well decide to turn your efforts to a squeakier wheel.

There are some simple tools that principals can use to begin to understand the apathy and even outright opposition to reform in the student support system. We believe that one of the most useful is *force-field analysis*, a technique that was first proposed by Kurt Lewin in the 1940s, which has long been a staple of change agents in the business sector.[1] Another is the SWOT (Strengths, Weaknesses, Opportunities, and Threats) analysis, which is often used as part of strategic planning. We will focus on the force-field technique here, because we believe that it generates clearer guides to action, but we have provided references about how to do a SWOT analysis at the end of the chapter.

The process of conducting a force-field analysis is not complex, but you may want to try it out with a trial group before working with others in the school. Force-field analysis works well with small or large groups. Remember that the facilitator must be a neutral figure and cannot inject opinions into the discussion, so you may want to recruit someone else for the role. This technique is among the best we know of to address the challenge of apathy.

What Is Force-Field Analysis?

A force-field analysis is based on the assumption that the people who work in schools are like the proverbial blind men and an elephant: Each

Figure 5.1 Sample Problem Statement: Need Better Use of Student Support Personnel

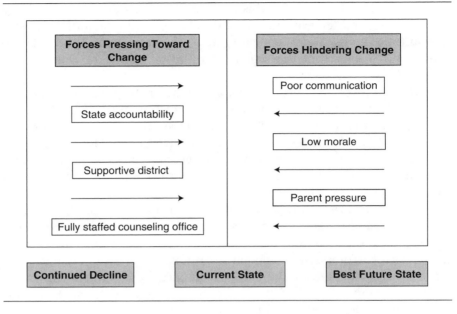

one feels different parts of the beast (in this case, the way in which the school is organized to promote student learning), but they don't see the same things. The goal of a force-field analysis is to put the insights from those who have grabbed hold of the elephant's tail with those who are patting its ears. Only when we understand the totality of the elephant—the systemic character of the school—can we prepare for change.

Force-field analysis encourages your staff to think about their school as a system—as an elephant rather than the discrete anatomical parts of an elephant—and how those parts work for and against the status quo. Its purpose is to help teams to look at the issues that they face as a function of two sets of offsetting factors. The essence of a force-field analysis is conveyed visually in Figure 5.1.

Force-field techniques can be used to frame existing problems or to anticipate factors that might emerge in the process of change. When it is used to define a problem more clearly, force-field analysis is helpful in pushing groups to pinpoint underlying issues in the school, such as morale, communication, effectiveness, and work climate. Force-field analysis also helps keep team members grounded in reality when they start planning a change by making them systematically anticipate what kind of resistance they could meet. Conducting a force-field analysis can build consensus by making it easy to discuss people's objections and then examining how to address these concerns.

How to Conduct a Force-Field Analysis

Conducting a force-field analysis is relatively straightforward. Here, we cover the basics so that you can see how simple it is.[2] More details and suggestions for performing this type of analysis are given in the resource section at the end of this chapter.

Step 1. State the problem or desired state and make sure that all team members understand it. You can construct the statement in terms of factors working for and against a desired state (if you all agree on an ideal) or in terms of factors working for and against the status quo or problem state (if you agree that there is a problem but not on the ideal state). Make sure that there is consensus and understanding at this point, or you will eventually have to start over!

Step 2. Brainstorm the positive and negative forces. You don't have to be definitive the first time around. You can add forces later in the discussion.

Step 3. Review and clarify each force or factor. What is behind each factor? What works to balance the situation? This discussion is very important and may allow you to add or change the factors that you have generated in Step 2.

Step 4. When you can reach consensus on a reasonable list of important factors, determine the strength of hindering forces (*high*, *medium*, or *low*) that prevent you from achieving the desired state or from improving the problem state. When the force-field model is used for problem analysis, the forces with the biggest impact should be tested as likely causes. If the force-field model is used to develop solutions, those factors with the biggest impact may become the focus of plans to reduce resistance to change.

Step 5. Develop an action plan to address the largest hindering forces.

Where you start with a force-field analysis depends to a great extent on your initial analysis of the existing energy and interest within the student support staff members. If they are raring to go, you should start by examining the state of the school's readiness to implement a renewed student support program like those described in Chapter 4. If support staff members are not committed to change, you need to examine the conditions within the student support system itself.

Alternative Ways to Reveal Barriers

Remember that the purpose of force-field analysis is, first, to analyze the present situation and, second, to determine some of the initial changes that may be required to smooth the path toward change. While we advocate force-field analysis as a tested approach for reaching these goals, it is not the only method. Its advantage is that it is relatively quick, can be carried out with large and small groups, and is easy to use with both school members and outside stakeholders. We believe that it is the best strategy in a school that already has an improvement program in place but in which the student support staff may be on the margins or inactive.

Force-field analysis may not be the best approach if your school is already engaged in a broad strategic planning process, in which case we would advise that you simply broaden whatever focus you already have to include attention to the student support staff as part of the larger initiative. An example would be a school in which teachers are already engaged in moving toward small schools-within-a-school, but where counselors and other student support members have only been involved in a limited way.

Alternatively, if you know that you need an all-school focus on enhanced student learning outcomes but have no current plan in place, it doesn't make sense to begin by focusing on student support. The case of Jack Partir, presented in Chapter 3, is an illustration of the kind of school that has been identified as failing to meet state standards for several years in a row, but at which there is no coherent plan for improvement. The principal knows that the problem lies in a deeply embedded set of attitudes and beliefs that can't possibly be altered by "fixing" his student support program. Student support is part of a larger issue in the school, and it is this barrier that needs attention. Again, if this is your school's situation, you should shift your thinking to include student support as a player in the broader design and planning process.

Finally, your school may be part of a larger, districtwide improvement initiative that uses other tools, such as a strategic planning SWOT analysis, which is often based on existing survey instruments and other more formal data gathering methods. There are many Web sites that provide a quick and free introduction on how to conduct a SWOT analysis (a recent Google search produced almost 400,000 sites), although we have some favorites that seem more applicable to a school setting.[3] The most important caution that we offer is that, no matter how tempting it is, don't conduct a SWOT analysis by yourself and present it to your staff. Its value, like that of the force-field analysis, is to unfreeze people's thinking about where they are and where they need to go.

Starting With Your Student Support Staff

We suggest using force-field or SWOT analysis with your student support staff—all of them, not just the counselors—before you begin to work with the rest of the school. Remember that one of the key elements of the new model of student support is to encourage leadership among counselors, social workers, and others who provide direct student services. Unless they feel that they are part of creating the environment for change, it will be difficult to ask them to become leaders at a later point.

On the other hand, we recommend that other stakeholder representatives be involved or consulted. The preliminary analysis in the force-field figure (Figure 5.1, p. 90) might, for example, have additional factors added if teachers, parents, or students were involved. Counselors and teachers who disagree about the forces might reveal underlying conditions that constitute a fundamental barrier. While it may seem too threatening to have "outsiders" involved in the first round of force-field analysis, you can bring others in later to confirm or to add to the work done by you and the student support staff.

Moving Toward Action

A force-field or SWOT analysis is not an action plan. Although it can help to uncover the hopes and fears of your staff members and other stakeholders, you need to be ready to step into a more active change process fairly quickly. At the same time, you and your student support staff need to be realistic: Making better use of your student support personnel may be critical to your school's long-term success in increasing student learning, but it is unlikely that it will be at the epicenter of your school's change activities. The dilemma that you are faced with is how best to (1) keep up the pressure and support for changing the role of the professionals outside the classroom who are working on student achievement, while (2) at the same time integrating changes in the student support activity into whatever core improvement program you are designing, and (3) making sure that others become the core leaders for this change so that you can focus on orchestrating and not micromanaging. This is the change master's job. We now consider some ways to pull off this balancing act as we move into the topic of working with the barriers that your team has uncovered.

The Limits to Force-Field and Other Types of Analyses

Following are some of the multidimensional characteristics of a problem evident in increasing the effectiveness of student support programs:

- **Lack of a Definitive Formulation.** The "problem of supporting student achievement" is defined in so many ways that it is not possible to arrive at a single, agreed-upon definition—even in a group of like-minded individuals.
- **Problem Interconnectedness.** Discussions of student support inevitably drift toward other social problems—such as family mobility, housing policies, transportation, and economic conditions. We cannot discuss improving the work of counselors and

social workers without running squarely into issues of school financing, poverty, immigration, and relationships with higher education (among others).

- **Dynamic and Uncertain Environments.** Improving student support must proceed in unstable settings. The tenure of school leaders—a major source of pressure and support for improvement in individual schools—is often brief. No one can predict what will happen with the multiple lawsuits that challenge current school financing and governance, or with efforts to counter federal and state accountability legislation.

- **Multiple Explanations for Every Aspect of the Problem.** Is the low performance of minority students due to racial and cultural issues, or to poverty? Would focusing on study skills induce higher cognitive development, or do you need to provide access to more rigorous courses? Do we need to work on the basics or on higher-order skills—and in what proportions?

- **Solutions Vary With the Diagnosis.** If the problem with student performance is racial and cultural, specialized support groups and family outreach might provide a key; if the issue is poverty and economic segregation, then assertively connecting with community resources becomes the priority.

- **No Definitive Way to Choose Among Solutions.** If we could experiment, we might find an answer to some dimensions of the problem. However, the most significant issues—such as race or poverty—are not amenable to valid and ethical experimentation.

- **Many Leverage Points.** Because the problems that students face in secondary schools are multidimensional, focusing on only one dimension is rarely possible or even desirable. From a practical perspective, every school is involved with multiple and overlapping improvement programs, even if they are not formally identified as such.

- **Lack of Closure.** Improving learning for all students is an open-ended problem. Even as we find that we are doing better in adolescent literacy, we can identify other areas of equal concern—core employability skills—that previously may not have been a high priority. Schools can always be improved.

These observations are not meant to instill a sense of hopelessness. But, it is important that you and the student support staff recognize that the process of diagnosis and planning is inevitably repetitive and recurrent. The force field that you identify this year—and the implied action steps—will be radically changed if there is, for example, an influx of non-English-speaking students into your schools or if fiscal conditions suddenly improve and permit you to hire additional staff. Be prepared to repeat your diagnoses on a regular, albeit informal, basis.

UNDERSTANDING WHAT IS NEEDED: WORKING ON THE PRECONDITIONS TO CREATE ACTION

When we use the term *preconditions,* we do not mean something that can be addressed and then filed away. Any initiative along the lines suggested here involves shaking up the existing system, and as change occurs, so does the need to revisit the status of the preconditions. What was clear and relevant at point X may seem muddy at point Y—once people have tried something that didn't work quite as planned. Skills are not acquired in a single training session, and as people become more adept, the need for additional skills actually increases. One of our favorite findings in studying school reform is that the longer principals have been involved in a major schoolwide change initiative, the longer they think it will take to reach their goal.[4]

Still, even if the process of change is continuous, you need to start somewhere. We have observed many efforts to change schools that start with a bang-up analysis of the problems and then fade into inaction because all of the energy was put into diagnosis and planning. So, we will begin at the beginning—as you contemplate the results of your preliminary analysis of pressures for and against change, but before any particular recommendations for change have been *solidified* in your school. At this stage, it is relevant to review the basic principles of moving from knowledge to action that we outlined in Chapter 1: *clarity, relevance, action images, will,* and *skill.*

Clarity and Relevance

Clarity and relevance can be difficult to separate in practice. Let's go back to the case of Chapter 3's Jack Partir, the principal whose counseling staff tended to blend into a school culture that was punitive in its orientation to students. While Jack had a personal vision of what student support should look like in his school, he had a difficult time communicating it to his staff—or us, for that matter. His principles—treat students and families with respect and assume that they are usually doing the best that they can—were a solid base for working with his particularly disadvantaged families, but his counselors didn't see how this should affect the way in which they organized their daily routines.

What could a thoughtful principal like Jack Partir do? First, we suggest that he needed help in writing out his beliefs and assumptions in order to engage in hard discussions with his staff about the disjuncture between what was happening in student support and a more ideal state. This statement would need to be realistic about the nature of the student population and would need to communicate his deep understanding of the psychology and development of young adolescents. He had commitment, but lacked a coherent statement of his vision.

Clarity and relevance must be context specific. The model of student support presented in Chapter 2 provides some guidelines, but it must be adapted to your school, its students, and the staff members who work with them. A highly idealized image that incorporates every element of the new role for student support might work if your staff members are already on the same page as you and the community is supportive of the school, but when vision and reality are separated by a chasm, the will to change can flounder. A more modest initial image might be required in a setting where the needs are greatest.

Action Images

Action images are the shared conceptual guides designed to replace existing structures and accepted patterns of behavior. The success of your reform efforts will be contingent on the relevance and effectiveness of the action images your team is able to create. The force-field exercise contributes by stimulating agreement about the barriers that must be addressed if change is to occur. Another way of creating more closely tailored action images for a traditional student support staff is through targeted professional development. The best strategy, when possible, is to send the staff out to observe a school that has a form of organization and service delivery that is more closely aligned with the perspectives of the ASCA model outlined in Chapter 2. If that is not possible, state professional conferences often have sessions on how the new model works in practice, and these will include action images your staff can share.

Probably the easiest way of creating action images for your school, however, is to brainstorm based on the images that we have set forth in Chapter 4. Your job is to get people to dream about the possible and to throw out ideas about how they could reorganize to be significantly better—and significantly different—than they are. We are particularly fond of a technique that we call "looking back on the future," discussed at the end of the chapter. Although Fred G. Thompson published a book with the same title in 1992, we have been using this tool ever since Matthew Miles, one of the fathers of organizational development in schools, introduced us to it two decades ago. This technique, like the force field, is simple to use and powerful. It involves a number of steps that ask people to imagine themselves in a future scenario where their ideal state has been achieved, and then to work backwards through an analysis of what was done to get there and, most important, the leadership they provided in the effort.

Richard Elmore refers to this idea as "backward mapping."[5] It is particularly helpful if you find yourself faced with in-the-box thinking about how to make student support programs work better. While such thinking can evidence itself in many ways, the most common are the following:

- Not wanting to give up any task that is currently being performed
- Thinking that the best solution is to add more people who are just like those who are already there
- Referring to an earlier "golden era" that may return at some point

Breaking out of the box is rarely done by exhortation alone, because only pushing harder does not alter the opposing forces that have created and sustained the equilibrium. The "looking back to the future" tool at the end of this chapter is designed to create action images to navigate through the barriers your staff now sees in common.

Issues of Will

When we talk about issues of will, we are putting a polite face on the problem of resistance. School principals must be willing to make people a bit uneasy, without being threatening. This is a political aspect to the job that not every principal is comfortable with. When we say "political," we don't suggest that you manipulate people for your own ends, but that you work with people to help them create their own discomfort with the status quo. Cryss Brunner, a University of Minnesota professor in the Education Administration and Policy Department, makes the important distinction between administrators who exercise *power over* people versus *power with* people.[6]

"Power over" people refers to the dictation of norms and behavior through dominance made possible in a hierarchical social structure. In its most extreme form, participants in a system characterized by dominance do not think about the problem, but rather think about how they are supposed to think about the problem. This is why threats can be counter productive: Subordinates become more focused on avoiding punishment than on finding the solution. "Power with" people is the crucial element that makes distributive leadership a more effective tool in change management. The application of these three concepts—power with people, distributive leadership, and change management—creates entrepreneurs within the system who share common goals because they helped to create those goals. They are able to work together to achieve those goals because their roles are expressed as action images.

Educators, including counselors, are rarely risk-takers or entrepreneurs. And certainly, the current policy climate, which has often resulted in blame being heaped on teachers and schools, has not helped. One of the most discouraging findings from Trish Hatch's national study of school counselors was that

school counselor perceptions with regard to their *professional legitimacy* has *increased* significantly from [1995 to 2002]. However, school counselors' perceptions of their *operational legitimacy* [as connected to the school operations and school reform] significantly *decreased* since the introduction of the ASCA National Standards. . . . Despite The Education Trust movement, the push of the professional organization through the development of the ASCA National Standards documents, and the culture within education for the past decade of school reform, . . . school counselors appear to have moved away from, instead of toward, participating in the educational reform movement.[7]

The desire to stay in a safe place, sheltered from the unceasing pressure to raise student performance, is a perfectly reasonable instinct. There are multiple ways of dealing with passive resistance that is based in fear. Here are just a few.

- **Demand Change and Step Back!** One way of getting people to move outside of their zone of comfort is to give them a job without an easy solution. You can simply tell the student support personnel that they can work together to design a new system to meet specified objectives (which you have identified because your principles and beliefs are clear and relevant), then give them the authority and a deadline. While risky, empowering a group of staff members while holding them accountable for producing provides a great incentive. This strategy will be discussed in more detail in the next chapter, under the topic of distributed leadership.
- **Use Allies.** Is there a faculty member in a local university who is on the same page and is willing to be supportive? Is there a member of the student support team who is more eager for change? If you have a new position for a counselor, can you hire someone whose approach to student support is similar to yours? Is there a teacher who wants more from student support and who would support new expectations for teachers?
- **Use Data to Make the Problems More Vivid.** There are already data that suggest that counseling is in trouble. Trish Hatch, a coauthor of the ASCA standards report, collected longitudinal data from counselors on how they spend their time, and showed that today's counselors spend *less* time on the activities advocated by their professional association than they did previously![8] She has allowed us to summarize some of her findings in one of the resources appended to this chapter. As we noted in Chapter 3, similar data are available for social workers. You could ask your student support group to analyze the findings and to explain why counselor and student behavior appears to be moving in the "wrong" or "right" direction.

- **Make Student Academic Life More Visible.** Another strategy is to have counselors collect their own data about the gap between what students want and what they experience. Have each member of the team shadow a typical student for a day, sitting through classes, lunch, and study hall, and interviewing the student about his or her aspirations and the barriers to achieving them. The exercise must include a prohibition on providing counseling or support: The purpose is just to live the student's life as he or she sees it. Even though counselors think that they understand the student experience, they rarely see it through the perspective of the student's life in school, and this can be a real eye-opener.

Issues of Skill

The first question that needs to be answered is whether your student support staff members have the skills necessary to develop and run a new-model program. We will not deal here with whether your staff is competent to carry out the core functions that were outlined in Chapter 2. It is likely, for example, that even if your staff is seasoned, they will not have the skills in data analysis needed to develop a system to monitor student progress in a timely fashion. If particular skills are lacking, you should be able to find the appropriate training at local universities or professional association meetings. We are more concerned here with the development of *metaskills,* which consist of related clusters of abilities garnered from work and educational experience that encourage a student support person to move beyond the narrow domain of a traditional job description. These skills will not be found in a single course, but need to be fostered and encouraged through reflection on the complex problems of practice.

As we noted in Chapter 3, one barrier to reorganizing student support in most schools is that it is currently a collection of diverse professionals who have different perspectives on what needs to be done to support student achievement. Furthermore, each of these groups has its own professional associations, own state and national meetings, and differentiated professional development opportunities. These are facts that cannot be changed by a principal. A principal can, however, help the members of the prospective team to look for the underlying and diverse skill set that is required to provide support for student learning and can create expectations that the range of needed skills will be developed by someone or some group.

Allocating responsibility for skill development is also one small step toward generating a comprehensive student support program in which the disciplines actively collaborate rather than merely cooperate when faced with a student crisis. You and your team may start with only a general vision that is short on particulars. As that vision does take form, your team will need the analytic skills to interpret observed practices and outcomes to assess the impact of evolving policies. This is the process of creating data-driven leaders and advocates, and it is where distributive leadership meets continuous improvement. You can also take this shorter version to heart:

- Conduct continuous internal monitoring.
- Conduct continuous external monitoring.
- Provide meaningful anchors by making work fun and reinforcing social connections within the team.

Your goal should be to help the student support personnel create a self-managing team that develops its own capacity to keep student support focused on the core goal of enhancing learning for all students with minimal direction from you. You will need to develop informal leadership within the group, and you must rely on your sense of who is able to think creatively and persuade others. Tapping the individuals who can do this, and rewarding them in whatever small ways you can, is important.

The skills needed to make a reformed student support system work may lie beyond the abilities that are central to each profession in isolation. A counselor may be superb at helping students to think about their academic careers within and beyond middle or high school, but may not be able to understand how to take advantage of a social worker's expertise in family-based interventions. The social worker may understand how to connect a child with social services, but then not work with teachers to negotiate a *system* of flexible expectations when there is a family crisis. The goal of an effective student support team is to create a whole-child model operating in a noncrisis environment that is still flexible enough to respond to the daily crises that do occur in schools. This requires not only the professional knowledge that each group brings to the job, but also a level of organizational integration and problem solving that is not generally taught in the masters programs in which they were trained. Just putting everyone on a team and telling them to work it out *may* not be sufficient.

This is where you come in. Frame the task so that the guidelines are clear. Work informally with the change agents on the team—the individuals who may have more experience or insight into how to make differentiated teams function effectively. As a licensed and experienced administrator, you will always maintain primary responsibility for issues of organizational design and planning.

CONCLUSION

Changing the way student support personnel operate in the school is a task that demands a great deal of upfront effort on your part if it is to succeed. We hope that you have a basic understanding of what needs to be done from Chapters 3 and 4, and that you will continue gathering information to further sharpen your own vision of the roles, functions, and desired outcomes of change. If you do not codevelop with your staff an understanding of the barriers to change and participate in working on the preconditions of clarity and relevance, action images, will, and skill, you may find that your later participation is less than effective. Your early participation in unfreezing and visioning is crucial in integrating professional disciplines that have not been cross-trained to work together.

We hope that our recommendations have had a positive and practical impact on you. We specifically wish that

- You have experienced a sense of urgency simply by paying attention to the issue and will ask people to meet about it.
- This sense of urgency has been accompanied by a vision of what student support might become.
- You have the confidence to begin developing a guiding coalition that includes all the people who will work together.
- You will help the team members to understand some—maybe not all—of the things that need to change.

Above all, we hope that the team you assemble will embrace your goals to the point that they will contribute enthusiastically to their own visions of how to reach them! With any major improvement activity in schools, there is a need to move quickly toward real change—something visible. So, we turn in the next chapter to the role that you can play in early implementation.

RESOURCES

Looking Back on the Future:
A Visioning Exercise for Improving Student Support

Instructions to the Facilitator

This activity requires a minimum of 45 minutes to be successful: approximately 25 minutes for the exercise and at least 20 minutes for sharing. Complete the full exercise before sharing. The point is to raise as many images of success as possible, and to surface the widest variety of leadership roles that people envision. Sharing before the exercise is over will tend to drive responses toward a common vision before alternatives are explored.

You will need to prepare four sheets of paper—one for each of the Reflections exercises shown below—for each participant. They should be handed out sequentially—in other words, people should *not* get the sheets as a packet that they can look over ahead of time.

It is important to get people to remember that they are playing a game and that they need to step outside of the way that they are feeling today. Instead, the point of this exercise is to get people to use their imaginations in a positive way. You know your group better than we do: Some groups can do this easily, while others are more resistant. If you have a resistant group, you should consider starting with a warm-up activity of some kind. You probably have encountered these from previous meetings. For example, you might

- Have everyone stand up and tell the person next to them one good thing that happened to them today and one bad thing.
- Have everyone stretch (you make up the stretching activity).
- Have everyone share a wish for one small thing that would make the world a better place.

Have people work on each of the four handouts, keeping close check on the time. This exercise does not work well if the pace is too slow, because then the gamelike aspect disappears and it begins to seem like work.

You will need blank paper available to record answers during the sharing period. If you have a large number of people, break them into groups of six or eight. Each group should have its own recorder. Groups should consist of people who fill different roles; don't let people cluster with their closest colleagues. If you do split into multiple groups, allow an extra 15 minutes to pool results with everyone.

Post the rules. Allow five minutes of discussion for Reflections II, III, and IV (the first reflection is just a warm-up exercise and doesn't need to be discussed). The parts should be treated in order, although people will want to undoubtedly move back and forth. The recorder should try to keep people within the allotted time and focused on the reflection at hand. The most useful way of doing this is to use a nominal group technique: Each person offers one point at a time until people run out of unique or new ideas.

Deal with resisters. Occasionally, people will resist this exercise, indicating that it is silly or not useful. Indicate ahead of time that people should feel free to leave the meeting if they are not able to make a productive contribution. If you believe that you are likely to get resistance, it may be useful to find an outside person (someone from the district office) to run the meeting. Obstructive behavior is often lessened in the presence of an outsider, and resisters are then more likely to become engaged and cooperative.

Manage the feedback. Tell people ahead of time what will happen with the ideas generated. There needs to be a clear plan for follow up. We suggest, at minimum, that the feedback notes be typed up (without attribution to any individual) and that you make a brief summary of what has been learned. This should be distributed to all participants.

What's the point? By observing the discussion, you will learn a great deal more about how people see themselves as making a contribution to this effort. You may be surprised at who comes up with good ideas. It is critical that, in the days after the exercise, you informally and verbally recognize people who were particularly helpful—those who might become good agents and spokespeople for the change. In addition, while some ideas may be real "pie in the sky," useful ideas about restructuring will emerge as well. These should be summarized and discussed, and at some point fed into the planning for change. When you finally do present the plan, you must remind people where the ideas came from; that is, you need to let people know that their work is having an impact even if they are not yet active players in the change process.

REFLECTION I

Getting Ready to Look Back (3 Minutes)

It is 2011 [substitute a date that is five years ahead of the current date] and you are having a celebratory dinner, having received the first state Award for Excellence in Supporting Student Learning. The award is based on three criteria:

- Effective integration of counseling, social work, and other support services into the school's academic work.
- Increased student achievement in three areas: attendance, student test scores, and student preparation for college and postsecondary success.
- Evidence of community involvement in supporting student learning and development.

Your group knew that they were on the right track five years ago, but none of them expected that their work would lead to becoming the national model for how to create a school that serves all the needs—academic, social, and personal—of students. As you look around the table at this group of people, some of whom you barely knew five years ago, you begin to reflect about your successes. . . .

The group of 12 people at dinner includes counselors, administrators, teachers, students, and a parent—some of whom initially were against the changes that led [name of your school] to receive the award and some of whom were early supporters. Who was there with you?

What are you wearing? It's time for dessert and you have ordered your favorite. What is it?

REFLECTION II

We Won Because. . . . (5 minutes)

It's 2011. Describe up to three important features of your school that you think helped it win the award. Please give some details, not just a single phrase.

1.

2.

3.

REFLECTION III

I Was a Key Player (5 minutes)

Although you didn't expect it, you were singled out in the awards ceremony for the role you played in helping transform [the name of your school].

What did you do that caught the attention of the State Award Team that came to look at your school's story? List the most important things. For each, give one or two specific illustrations of what you did.

1.

2.

3.

REFLECTION IV

It Wasn't Easy (3 minutes)

We know that winning this award has meant hard work for everyone. What were the three major challenges you faced along the way?

1.

2.

3.

Of course, the reflections are fantasy exercises. For every hero that is recognized, a hundred are not. But we are all actors in our own social dramas and even if the conclusion to the plot is not the medal of excellence hung on your neck during prime time, children turned into young adults better prepared for life and citizenship is a better reality anyway.

Our Favorite Web Site for Problem-Solving Tools for Nonprofit Organizations

Sometimes, the best things in life are free! Although we recommend all of the books that were listed in Chapter 1, none of them will provide you with a lot of assistance on specific change strategies. For that, you should visit a Web site sponsored by UNICEF and Management Sciences for Health (erc.msh.org/quality/pssum.cfm). This site includes a variety of easily accessible tools, discussed on the next page, for each of the stages of change that we discuss in this chapter.

Identifying and Describing Problems

This book assumes that you agree with our observation that student support services in most schools are not well organized to provide leadership in initiatives with student achievement. Nevertheless, there is still work to be done to get to a definition of the problem that is specific to *your school* and *your staff members*:

> A problem occurs when there is a difference between what "should be" and what "is"; between the ideal and the actual situation. A problem
>
> - expresses the difference between the hoped for and the actual situation;
> - is directly or indirectly related to the health of the population;
> - is expressed in terms of processes, effects, impacts, and satisfaction."[9]

Systematizing or Analyzing the Causes of Problems

Force-field analysis, which we have described in detail, is also one of the techniques described on this Web site, but, as we have noted, it is not the only one. You will find other guides to help you reach the following goal:

> Redefining the problem: you need a clear idea of the problem so that it can be analyzed. Revisit the questions of problem description to make sure you are clear about the following:
>
> - What is the problem about?
> - How frequently does it occur?
> - When and where does it occur?
> - Who is affected?[10]

Planning a Solution

Your initial force-field analysis of factors influencing student support will point directly to some elements of a solution specific to your school. In addition to the approaches that we identify in this book, you will find others on the UNICEF/Management Sciences for Health Web site related to the goal of creating your own school-specific strategy for change:

> It is likely that several alternatives for solving the problem exist. However, the "best" strategy depends on the forces that impede or favor the change, and the effectiveness and cost of the alternative solutions.[11]

Implementing and Evaluating the Changes

This Web site emphasizes the use of tools designed for business based on Deming's total quality management principles.[12] Its recommendations and descriptions are, however, adapted for nonprofit institutions and are relatively simple to use. The emphasis of the Web site is clearly related to our message:

> To implement the solution, the team members require specific technical skills and support from the managers.[13]

A monitoring system is the sum of all procedures used continuously to evaluate a program and to provide information about its purpose, objectives, activities, impact, costs, and user satisfaction. . . . You need a set of tools to measure the relationship between the expected results and the actual results. The difference will determine the need for corrective measures, and which ones to apply.[14]

We particularly like the simple introduction to prioritization and control charts, which are very helpful in monitoring and evaluating implementation.

A Short Summary of *National Standards for School Counseling Programs: A Source of Legitimacy or of Reform?*[15]

Despite attempts to educate my administrators, I still get stuck in non-counseling duties.

It is very discouraging to have the National Standards available and yet have an administration that really doesn't care much about these standards. . . . The administration does not see the value in the work I do.

Administration has to accept the same standards or it isn't going to work.

In her research, Patricia Hatch compares the responses of a school counseling survey given in 1995 with the responses given in 2002. Eighty-three percent of the respondents of the 2002 survey indicated they were aware of the ASCA National Standards. Three goals of the survey research were to examine "the extent to which the ASCA National Standards have served to more clearly define role and function, changed school counselors' beliefs and behaviors with regard to the performance of counseling and non-counseling activities and have positively impacted school counselors' perceptions regarding the legitimacy of their profession."[16] Her research, in effect, asks if the awareness of new standards is, by itself, a powerful way to begin to change the role of the school counselor.

The answer to the question appears to be no. Specifically, Hatch asked if beliefs and behaviors with regard to the performance of counseling and noncounseling activities changed with the introduction of the ASCA standards in 1995. As we stated in Chapter 5, she actually found that school counselors view certain ASCA-associated activities as less important in 2002 than they did in 1995. For example, the following items were ranked *less important* in 2002 than in 1995:

- Consultation with teachers and parents
- Staff development
- Collaborating with community agencies
- Providing staff development programs for teachers

And the following factors were ranked *significantly less important* in 2002 than in 1995:

- Consulting with faculty, staff, and administration
- Collaborating with community agencies on student referrals
- Participating in school/district reform initiatives
- Conducting parent workshops
- Coordinating advisory programs
- Providing staff development

This surprising result shows that even though a newer model exists, it still takes time for those new beliefs and behaviors to actually become embedded into the everyday lives of school counselors. Knowledge, by itself, may make little headway against forces maintaining the status quo, or even in pressing actual practice in a direction away from clearly stated goals. The quotations at the beginning of this section suggest that some of the inconsistencies she found in beliefs and behaviors between 1995 and 2002 might exist because of the lack of administrator understanding and support.

In addition, the following items were listed as *less important* but ranked high in counselor behavior—indicating that even though counselors do not believe these functions should be a part of their job, they spend a significant amount of time doing them anyway:

- Organizing and conducting standardized achievement and aptitude inventories
- Managing grade reporting and student rank in class
- Planning and managing academic programs of study

Equally important and surprising, counselors ranked the following items as *more important* in the 2002 survey than they did in 1995:

- Participating in other school duties, such as bus duty, playground duty, lunch duty, and hall duty
- Assisting in school assembly programs
- Facilitating student placement

Clearly, counselors are still struggling with beliefs about their role working to link those beliefs with work behavior. School counselors will need more than a national model to fully embrace change. Again, the quotations we began this section with suggest that counselors are looking for and need a strong administrative leader to guide them in the implementation of the ASCA model. Having knowledge of the new model and its components is not enough, but it does have some very significant benefits. For instance, Hatch, in her research, drew the following conclusions:

- "School counselors who have knowledge of the standards document or whose institution (i.e., administrator and school board) has knowledge are significantly more likely to monitor and use data in the development of their programs. Those who only attended a training or conference on the ASCA National Standards are not."
- "School counselors who have knowledge of the standards document, who attend trainings or conferences on the ASCA National Standards, or whose institution (i.e., administrator and school board) has knowledge are significantly more likely to write a mission statement, develop program goals, identify student competencies and align their programs with the state content standards."
- "School counselors who have knowledge of the standards document or whose institution (i.e., administrator and school board) has knowledge are significantly more likely than those who only attended a training or conference on the ASCA National Standards, to have administrative support for their programs."
- "School counselors who have knowledge of the standards document, who attend trainings or conferences on the ASCA National Standards, or whose institution (i.e., administrator and school board) has knowledge are significantly more likely to use data to measure and share the results of their programs for students"[17]

Finally, Hatch revealed that even though school counselors' perceptions of having professional legitimacy have increased since 1995, their perceptions of their operational legitimacy have actually decreased. From this, we can conclude that school counselors see themselves as less involved in schoolwide reforms and less important to the systemic operations of schools than they did in 1995. These findings are consistent with our research, and indicate an even greater need for administrators to begin to include all student support professionals into the overall school reform agenda.

Initiating and Sustaining Change

6

In this chapter you will

- Be shown tested strategies for introducing complex changes.
- Learn some mechanisms to keep change on track.
- Consider some ways of avoiding big failures while encouraging risk.
- Think about what this means for your leadership role.

The performance dip model introduced in Chapter 1 predicts that any change in an institutional setting will usually make things worse before they improve. This is especially true when altering established structures that deal with a so-called wicked problem—and this certainly includes student support issues and goals. In Chapter 5, we suggested some ways to analyze your current system of student support. In this chapter, we consider strategies for introducing change and starting on the process for continuous improvement of your student development support system.

We emphasize again that the issue of student support addresses a particularly wicked problem for schools and school administrators. As such, some of the standard recommendations for initiating change may not work. We begin, thus, with some practical principles to keep in mind.

PRACTICAL PRINCIPLES

First, Stir the Pot

One assumption that has been affirmed over and over again in looking at successful educational change masters is that they are more oriented to action than contemplation. This stands in contrast to most people, who prefer extended speculation on various scenarios and problems until they are confident of a prospective outcome. The drawback of this approach is that there are always unintended and unexpected consequences—good and bad—that can undermine your extensive preplanning. Break free of this trap by modeling an action component and involving others early on. You and your coleaders can start with something low cost and low risk that demonstrates your serious intent without threatening the status quo. Kotter, in his popular book on business change, calls attention to this by looking at the need for short-term wins.[1] But how do you do that in schools, where the bottom line—student achievement—is poorly measured through annual tests that don't provide easy ways to determine which variables have influenced your results? Here are some suggestions based on our studies of effective principal change masters.

Act—Then Plan

An easy and visible way to show your intent is to involve student support personnel in all professional development that is focused on improving curriculum and teaching practices. It is likely that this has not happened before, and it demonstrates to everyone that change is in the wind without threatening anyone's comfort level. If counselors know about the curricular innovations, they will be better prepared to discuss them with students and teachers when issues inevitably arise. Best of all, you don't need a long-term plan in place to do this.

If you have new resources or a hiring opportunity due to a retirement or departure, you can use your position as the school's human resources leader to make a statement. If there is an open position or an employee whose workload has some slack, use them to assist student support personnel with the more mundane and less specialized tasks they have acquired over the years. And, if you want to make a real statement, have an administrator drive material to the central office rather than sending a counselor!

Another low-cost option is to ask your student support professionals to develop a written job description for their roles. Rather than the list of functions "as assigned," ask them to *clearly allocate time to each activity and indicate if they feel that time is well spent.* They should not, at this point, be individualized, but can be role specific to each profession represented on your student support staff. After reviewing them, arrange for a presentation to the rest of the staff. This exercise requires the individuals performing the jobs to think about what they do and how much time is spent on each activity while, at the same time, it informs the rest of the staff about the nature of the support staff's invisible roles.

These actions are not dramatic or complex, but each reinforces your position: Change will occur, and it will be based on thoughtful involvement and expansion of the student support role.

Adjust the Decision-Making and Communication Structures

A slightly more radical change that you can make with minimal consultation is to include a student support professional, perhaps the head of the counseling department, on your administrative team. If your district or school is already moving toward a more broadly based administrative team, this may not even be seen as radical. We find, however, in looking at many school Web sites that the inclusion of counselors or social workers is still relatively rare. The point of such a move is to reinforce the broader leadership and advocacy role that you are preparing student support personnel to take.

- **Suggestion:** If you have not come very far in terms of shared decision making, use visible, informal methods to consult with your support personnel. Have lunch with the student support group once a week. Reach out to indicate that their opinions matter.
- **Suggestion:** Place a student support representative on major school improvement task forces and teams, even if it is not clear yet how their work will intersect with the school's academic planning. You will be creating the expectation that they have a part to play in reform, even if no one is quite sure yet what that role looks like.

Begin Developing Student Support Indicators

Developing student support indicators will be an ongoing task; continuous improvement requires continuous measurement. Involve your student support staff in creating indicators that measure real progress, not just numbers of students seen or tasks undertaken. Start slowly as you build consensus; a set of goals with measurable milestones will motivate your staff from within. This is still an early step, but it forces your support staff to focus on results—measuring as well as producing.

- **Suggestion:** Have student support staff develop a calendar of events for the next year—and make it available for all staff to see so that they are held accountable to others. There's nothing like a deadline for presenting to someone else to sharpen thinking!
- **Suggestion:** You can use the calendar to help the staff think about progress and adjustments needed along the way.
- **Suggestion:** Identify and tabulate indicators that measure the social health of your school. Remember Principal Stuart Long and his goal of reducing absenteeism, from Chapter 4. What do you want to see more of? What do you want to see less of? Track participation in extracurricular activities as well as hours spent in detention. Challenge your staff: Ask, How do we create goals that measure real progress rather than manipulate figures?

Find Supporters and Build Commitment Among Teachers

Use "hall talk" or other informal means to find a few teachers who understand that student support can make their job easier.

- **Suggestion:** When you are chatting with teachers, see if any have considered switching to counseling as a career. Such a teacher would be an obvious choice to act as a liaison with the student support office. This would serve as a professional development goal for the teacher while encouraging communication between teachers and support staff.

These above-listed actions are *not* the change program. They are merely signals to the rest of the school and other stakeholders that you are serious and willing to put yourself on the line. Change is not easy, and any of these activities may create push-back from people inside and outside your student support team. But since these actions don't yet pose serious challenges to the status quo, they are more likely to be received as evidence of your intentions while stimulating energy among those who agree that change is needed.

Initiate Real Change at the Periphery

The periphery is where the web of change begins to take shape. So far, you have not asked anyone to alter what they do to any great extent. You have been laying the groundwork. Now, others need to become more active as you continue to provide support—and maybe a little pressure as well.

The current conventional wisdom of school reform initiatives is that, in order to have an effect, they must touch the whole school. We agree with the assumption that real increases in student learning will not occur by only tinkering around the edges, and we also know that small innovations that affect few people are often easily implemented but easily discontinued. Peripheral changes are all too frequently discontinued as soon as the initial enthusiasm fades or when the first tear in the improvement web discourages efforts in other components of the change endeavor. But a whole-school reform is made up of hundreds of smaller change initiatives that are linked together in ways that may be better imagined as a spider's web rather than a road map. Some of these initiatives are directly linked to the core activity of the school—teaching and learning in the classroom. Others, like changing the school's schedule or developing stronger professional learning communities, are required in order to support classroom change.

The 10% solution is no small initiative, but it is unlikely that teachers will initially view it as central to their work. It can be developed and nurtured in its early stages without making big demands on all staff members.

This allows you to initiate change in a way that demonstrates that the 10% solution will really be a solution and not another burden. It is also consistent with the best advice that is offered to change managers by the Harvard Business School:

> The likelihood of success is greatest when change is initiated in small, fairly autonomous units. . . . Once change is accomplished and witnessed [by others], diffusion of the change activity throughout the organization is more likely.[2]

The implication of this advice is to begin by changing the student support program work without involving a lot of the other school staff. This recommendation holds whether your student support staff are ready to go, or more cautious. Just because some are committed doesn't mean that they are ready to engage the rest of the school.

Your initial task is, therefore, to help the support staff learn how to become leaders and advocates consistent with the examples in Chapters 2 and 4. Our research suggests that most practicing counselors, even when they support this new role, don't really understand what it entails. You, as the guide and supervisor of the school, have far more experience, even if you don't feel that you are an expert. Your job is to coach them to initiate change from below. They need your support and your affirmation: Principals are, after all, viewed by everyone as the gatekeepers who determine which new ideas are appropriate for their school.[3] Here are some actions that you can take.

Focus on Data-Based Decision Making

With some support, counselors and other student support professionals can begin to gather data from students, parents, and teachers. Although needs assessments are a popular tool for gathering stakeholder input, we do not recommend a major effort of this type prior to making your initial changes. We believe that including stakeholders in any activity sets up expectations for further involvement that you probably can't meet at this point. In addition, major needs assessments chew up a lot of time and energy, and therefore postpone efforts to change behavior within the school. Finally, the most important step is to encourage your student support professionals to be more student driven and responsive, even if they don't know *exactly* what the student needs. The point of data-based decision making is to find and act on data as it becomes available, and not necessarily to wait for perfect information.

Every professional staff member has ideas—often repressed—about ways in which student needs are not being well served. If these ideas can be surfaced and discussed, they can serve as guides for your initial efforts to gather data. The staff members won't have all of the answers, but different members may have different pieces of the answer. If you can encourage them to gather information that is relevant to their concerns about the match between what they do and what resources and support students should have, they will be on the road to data-based decision making.

- **Suggestion:** Conduct a *limited* student survey on a topic of concern to the student support staff—for example, if 10th graders understand what they need to do to graduate, or whether seniors have realistic postsecondary plans. A sample survey is included in the resources section at the end of this chapter.
- **Suggestion:** Use the collection of data as a lever to introduce the broader issue of making student support more data driven. Ensure that your suggestions are backed up with technical assistance or professional development—most counselors and social workers will not be experienced with data analysis.
- **Suggestion:** Professional development should come from within the student support office if you have people with data analysis skills. Use your internal resources!

Data collection and evaluation should begin as an internal evaluation to reduce the anxiety that some surprises might induce. Emphasize that you cannot improve as a group until you can document what is not working. Involve your entire staff in considering what kind of data will be useful, and then make sure you are not duplicating the efforts of some other group in your school or at the district level.

- **Suggestion:** Assign one person overall responsibility for keeping track of data collection efforts to reduce overlap and stimulate use.

USING A SURVEY TO ASSESS STUDENT NEEDS

In a large urban school district, all high school guidance counselors collaborated to conduct a survey to assess 9th-grade needs. The counselors believed they needed current information on what new high school students need in order to prioritize their work. They also cut down on paperwork by integrating their questions on an existing survey already in the works—an early signal for collaboration.

Examples of questions included the following:

- I know what I need to do to graduate from high school.
- I feel that I am a part of this school.

- I have met with a counselor individually or in a group setting about the following _____.
- I would like to talk to someone about the following _____.

The results of the survey showed that

- 90.7% of students said they knew what they needed to do to graduate. This result indicated that guidance counselors were doing a great job in this area. Therefore, the guidance counselors knew they could shift their attention to other matters that the students said were of concern to them.
- 15.9% of students indicated that they do not feel like they are a part of the school.
- Many students indicated that they had never met with a counselor (45.3% individually and 55.9% in a group setting).

As a result, the districtwide survey helped student support staff focus on specific areas of need. For example, 41.4% of the students indicated that they would like to talk more about creating a plan for high school and beyond. One way the district responded to this information was to create an online tool for all high school students to use called The Six-Year Plan. This Web site allows students to input all of their classes to make sure they are on track to graduate. In addition, the site has places where students can look for information on careers as well as college and university requirements. The Web site offered students an opportunity to think about their future after school and to consider their academic plans as part of their overall goals.

Use Internal Assessment Tools

After taking the first steps toward data collection and data use, you can build on earlier efforts to create collective accountability for student support by looking for indicators of group success. An important feature of bottom-up assessment design is that your student support staff—or at least most of them—will agree that the indicators are relevant for assessing their work if they participate in identifying them. There is considerable evidence suggesting that when professionals know, understand, and agree with assessment measures, they then find assessment more rewarding than anxiety producing. The most effective pressure a change master can apply in a situation of distributive leadership is the establishment of agreed-upon standards to measure success, whether they are standards for school or individual performance.

The creation of performance standards also forces your staff to focus on results, rather than on new activities that may not effectively complement overall school goals. We agree with research suggesting that closer supervision (but not micromanaging) builds support and pressure for improved performance.[4]

- **Suggestion:** Make sure that you don't just change a few words on teacher assessment models to apply them to student support. The models need to be clear and reflect the new vision of your student support model.
- **Suggestion:** Work with the team to study publicly available examples of student support assessment instruments in order to design one that meets your needs. Two publicly available but very different counseling models—one more qualitative and narrative, the other using quantitative rating scales—are easily accessible on the Web. One was developed by the Fayette County Public Schools, Lexington, Kentucky, (www.fayette.k12.ky.us/forms/pd/certeval/guidance-data.doc) and the other by the Department of Public Instruction in North Carolina (www.cabarrus.k12.nc.us/pdf/SchoolCounsler PA.pdf).

Engage in Visioning With the Student Support Team—Again!

This process of transformation began with an analysis of existing student support conditions. Part of this included speculating with your staff about some ideal future state, but that early discussion falls short of a real vision. At this point in the process, you will have more data and may even see results from some early changes. Now, it is time to reexamine that initial vision, creating something more elaborate and realistic with specific goals.

You can assume that an effective 10% solution will require more than just tweaking the existing student support structure. Only a complete reorganization will prevent the old ecology of job expectations from reasserting itself. The student support staff must begin to develop their own image of reorganizing their work, one based in function (as demonstrated in the examples in Chapters 2 and 4) rather than traditional roles we described in Chapters 1 and 3. You can help by changing some structures yourself and by allowing your staff some flexibility in this reorganization. But remember, you need a committed student support staff if change and restructuring will ever evolve into a real solution.

- **Suggestion:** If you feel ill-equipped and the district cannot help you to support the team in organizational/job redesign, look for a faculty member or advanced graduate student from a local university who is willing to work with the student support team to facilitate the process.

- **Suggestion:** Be creative in looking for help; many business schools, for example, require that their MBA students engage in real-life projects as part of their training.

Encourage Personal Leadership
Through Professional Development Plans

Many districts now require teachers and principals to develop annual professional development plans (PDPs) and assess the degree to which appropriate progress is being made toward increased knowledge and skills. As with many reforms in American education in the past few decades, however, student support personnel have been largely overlooked in this kind of approach to improvement at the individual level. A personal PDP should include training and coursework that focuses on ASCA-based models. It should also be explicitly tied to school improvement goals and to district or state student learning standards. Let your student support staff know they will be evaluated on the basis of how well they have availed themselves of professional opportunities.

- **Suggestion:** Keep on the lookout for a book by Shelton and James on PDP for counselors, forthcoming from Sage. In addition, check out www.fcps.net/forms/pd/certeval/guidance-data.doc for resources. Some teacher-focused sites, such as www.ncrel.org/sdrs, may also be useful guides.

Encourage Small-Scale Changes and Action Research

Do not let this energy dissipate by waiting for the perfect plan! Remind your staff that continuous improvement is all about making changes, studying their efforts, and then making more changes. Most teachers are familiar with this idea of action research, which emphasizes the importance of understanding why a new effort succeeded or failed. This concept easily extends to student support staff as well.

When teachers are asked what makes principals supportive, they usually talk about a low-risk environment in the school. They want to feel that trying out new ideas is rewarded, even when they don't work. They need to be able to learn from small failures—something that research suggests is critical to adult development. As one study of problem solving "on the shop floor" found,

> Problem-solving processes benefit from rich data that capture multiple perspectives on a problem; problem categories that are "fuzzy"; and organizational structures that facilitate the development of a common language for discussing problems. Also, when problems

are framed as opportunities for learning, the combination of positive attributions that boost motivation and the suppression of threat effects can increase the effectiveness of improvement activities.[5]

Unanalyzed small failures can add up to major collapse, as examination of NASA disasters has demonstrated.[6] The key to effective leadership in a low-risk, high-change school is to ensure that change is always accompanied by measurement and assessment—the tools of continuous improvement.

This is where action research is relevant. Curiously, though, most of the literature on action research assumes that the principal is out of the picture. We disagree with this premise, noting that every study of leadership and change in schools suggests that principals need to be active members of the improvement cycle, even when they lack specific expertise. Principals who are eager to learn and to acknowledge that imperfection is a consequence of change are more likely to become an essential component of action research and focus on professional inquiry.

- **Suggestion:** Initiate a schoolwide discussion on action research that is currently being considered or ongoing, and encourage one or two student support staff members to introduce a project of their own.

Change at the periphery can begin with the student support personnel and a few volunteer teachers. Any real innovation will create ripples through the rest of the school, which you, as change master, have the opportunity to build on. Beginning at the periphery does not imply that the effects of change will be contained there, but momentum will not build on its own accord. Moving student support from outside of the web of school reform to the edge of school reform is only the first step toward your goal of complete integration.

BEGIN REAL CHANGE, REFINE THE PLAN, AND ENGAGE OTHERS

Starting small at the periphery is not without its risks. We all know one old scenario of failed change in schools: Someone announces that "we need some changes around here" and appoints a committee to work on it. The committee members go to work, fitting the task in as best they can between their regular responsibilities. Because they are busy and their work is often interrupted, they don't have much time to talk to other teachers in the school. Six months later, they have a solution, which is roundly voted down by the rest of the faculty as just plain stupid. It doesn't work, but the scenario keeps on repeating itself. Your job as change master is to nurture these changes at the periphery. This means that you must both support early enthusiasts to press on and use your role as chief administrator to dissolve resistance.

Change is like turning over a different rock on a daily basis: You never know what will be underneath. Conducting a force-field analysis (or other diagnostic process) and working on the preconditions will reveal issues facing your school that have not been fully confronted. At the same time, however, if you have been providing support and putting a bit of pressure on your student support team and their colleagues, some real plans for changing the organization and activities of student support will emerge, as will a continuously refined vision of what the school could become. Now it is time to manage the performance dip!

We deliberately use the word "manage" rather than "solve." The problems addressed by student support are inherently difficult, and they not only defy easy solutions, but also any solution. The management response we recommend is deep coping. *Depth* means thinking structurally in terms of capacity building rather than in a "push a little harder" or "fire fighting" style. Sure, it is better to drain the swamp rather than fight the alligators one by one, but what if the swamp cannot be drained? Magic solutions do not exist for wicked problems. In-depth coping demands multiple creative strategies: There is no single solution—but this response makes for a more manageable problem.

Identify Problems Early

Anticipating problems before they become crises will be both the most important and most unappreciated leadership task that you face. Schools that fail in their reform efforts often fail to actively look for problems or, even if the problems are identified, don't talk about them until they are full blown. People rarely notice a small problem that was dealt with before it became huge. There is rarely anyone in a school who is better placed to take on this task of problem finding than the principal or designated coordinator.

One of the most interesting findings in Louis and Miles' study of high schools was that the principals in schools that were making good progress on change reported that they had encountered more problems in implementation, but had a larger repertoire of strategies for handling them.[7] Effective principals addressed all aspects of a problem, from the how-to-get-it-done technical aspects through cultural issues of communication and dispute resolutions to the bare-knuckle politics of district policies or union pressures. That study concluded,

> "Go thou and cope better" is not a useful commandment. Rather, better coping is more likely when certain preconditions have been working out. These include a coherent, shared vision, a stance toward coping that stresses learning from experience, strong support for

implementation efforts, adequate time and energy set aside for coping through regular meetings; use of external assistance to expand the coping repertoire and extend skills; and deep coping itself—as a way of mobilizing further good coping through durable structures.[8]

Set aside time to identify and discuss problems that are likely to lead you off track during the initial phases of introducing new activities—and do so in ways that are visible to people outside of the student support offices.

Choose a Role and Be Clear About It

There are two roles for a principal in a change effort of this magnitude. The first is as *orchestrator*. This involves supporting gradual, organic change in which others assume the most visible leadership roles. The second requires you to take on a more visible role as an *active champion*.

Orchestrating is always the preferred route—when conditions allow it. If the members of your student support staff are energized, have a plan for reorganizing their own activities and relationships, and have created a sense of team endeavors directed toward a new vision of student support, you can step back to monitor and support their efforts. We have observed schools with an active counseling staff in which leaders have emerged to take on the task of changing the minds and hearts of the rest of the school. They can and do succeed, as the example of Truman High School in Chapter 4 demonstrates. This kind of leadership for change has worked in many systems and under a variety of circumstances. Orchestration is a natural fit with distributed leadership.

Championing is an alternative that is required under less desirable scenarios. If your support staff is ambivalent about where they want to go and if the teachers are content with the status quo, or if there is a history of friction between student support staff and other members of the school, you need to step up your presence. As a principal, you have greater visibility and influence in a school, even when you work with persuasion rather than simply "telling and selling." The latter point is important: telling and selling alone, without active persuasion and modeling, can run counter to the school support team's efforts to use dialogue and volunteerism to spread the vision that they can support classroom practice and learning in new ways.

Orchestration may be preferred, but your pressure for change may need to be sustained if there are lingering doubts among the teachers, student support staff, or the district office.

Formalize Efforts to Create a Leadership Group

Earlier we suggested getting at least one teacher to work as a liaison to the student support staff. Now, it is time to name a short-term task force that includes a few more teachers and perhaps even a parent. The goal here is providing understanding and commitment, while not asking for a great deal of effort at this time. The members of the task force will keep the issue in view, without being threatening, and should remain aware that they are the cadre of change agents for the whole school. As teachers and student support personnel work together on common improvement goals, they will serve as role models for bridging the gulf that normally separates their working roles.

- **Suggestion:** Use the task force to develop a strategic plan for creating closer linkages between student support and classrooms. A report highlighting changes that are needed by both teachers and student support personnel should then be shared with the entire staff.

GUIDELINES FOR THE ADMINISTRATIVE ADVOCATE

Whether orchestrator or champion, you will need to play a strong transformational role in the change effort, in addition to managing the inevitable daily problems. Our own research and the research of others has convinced us there is no simple five- or seven-step process of change that will ensure success: Remember, you inhabit the world of wicked problems. Nonetheless, there are some general guidelines for moving a change from the periphery into the core.

1. **Help Your People Decide What to Discard as They Move Ahead.** Ron Heifetz, a Harvard professor who writes extensively about change, argues that leadership means dealing with losses and addressing the fundamental question, "What's essential and what's expendable?"[9] People who work to serve the needs of children are rarely willing to let go of any task they believe could help. But, in order to refocus student support on core achievement goals, some activities—even important activities, such as running grief groups or riding with students to the hospital when they are hurt—may have to be shifted from the current counseling and social work staff. The school administrator must be prepared to support and ultimately take responsibility for shedding valuable activities that can no longer be sustained.

2. **Help Your People Adapt to Uncertain Settings.** Heifetz also contrasts leaders who exude confidence by living in the certainties of a world that no longer exists with "adaptive leaders" who show people how to deal with uncertainty.[10] His central tenet is that we live in settings with competing organizational values that facilitate new ways of organizing around a common goal. He argues that this involves a major shift in the way we think about leadership (see Figure 6.1).

Figure 6.1 Values and Leadership

TECHNICAL VALUES (Silverback Leadership)
vs.
ADAPTIVE VALUES (True Leadership)

DIRECTION
Where are the berries?
vs.
What do we do when there are no berries or when we come under attack
from a new adversary?

PROTECTION
Circle the wagons, stick head in the sand, call out the National Guard.
vs.
Create a new approach to defending the constituency through a new
understanding of its nature.

ROLE ORIENTATION
Hierarchy of most valuable and most powerful current members.
vs.
Define importance of all constituents and the band's role in
the larger community.

CONTROLLING CONFLICT
End fights that threaten group social order.
vs.
Elicit diversity of views in order to strengthen group.

NORM MAINTENANCE
Punish violators of social norms.
vs.
Set personal example and seek to broaden social norms to
include useful alternatives.

3. **Help Your People Gain Access to the Knowledge and Skills They Will Need.** Principals often act as gatekeepers to professional development opportunities. Effective principals spread the word through hall talk and informal communication, and they use their networks to scan for resources that will provide learning opportunities for the staff. Effective change leaders listen for indicators of what their people need and then connect them to resources outside the school. Part of a principal's job is to look beyond the school, the district, and even the state in order to tap into inventions and ideas from across the world. Fortunately, with the advent of Google and the Internet, this is easier now than ever before.

4. **Balance Leadership and Delegation.** Leadership in a learning organization is subtle and unstable. The literature suggests that effective change requires a principal who can be a champion or an

orchestrator, as conditions dictate. In addition, there is the tricky question of how to encourage teacher leadership without undermining pedagogy and the focus on classroom work.

THE CHANGE MASTER
AND DISTRIBUTED LEADERSHIP

Distributed leadership is a new phrase that is becoming widespread among educational administrators, but it is not an entirely new concept. The term, while variously defined, encapsulates the notion that creating effective schools requires more than strong role-centered leadership (e.g., the principal or the superintendent). Instead, the complexity of school environments demands a broader sharing of ownership and responsibility, including key decisions and tasks. The concept of change master is ideally suited to describing the principal's role in facilitating this kind of fundamental reorganization of job expectations and relationships.

Educational professionals are increasingly asked to make changes in their work lives: making more professional decisions about their work, expanding notions of responsibility, and decentralizing authority from remote to local sites of practice. These changes do not just happen; they require a leader to reconfigure how responsibility for decision making is allocated.

As you move toward a real change in the organization of your school's student support system, you will need to rethink your own leadership role. Your job is too complex to take on the responsibility for orchestrating the design and building of the entire webbed network that will ultimately constitute your efforts to improve student learning without making use of the concepts of distributed leadership. The teacher leadership literature discusses leadership roles exercised by those who are not in formal positions of authority.[11] Smylie, Conley, and Marks point out in a review of new approaches to leadership that distributed leadership stresses the importance of shifting our "attention away from individual and role-based conceptions of leadership and toward organizational and task-oriented conceptions of leadership."[12] It is increasingly imperative that principal leadership is exercised as an organization-wide resource of power and influence.

With its initial roots in the teacher empowerment research, however, empirical research on distributed leadership in schools has been largely confined to examining how leadership is shared between administrators and teachers. The cause of this oversight is the same reason that student support professionals have largely escaped accountability in educational reform: They are viewed as ancillary rather than central to the schools primary mission of student achievement.

According to Pounder, Ogawa, and Adams, the multidirectional and fluid nature of social influence can affect the performance of the school in different ways.[13] The orientation of distributed leadership assumes that individuals in positions of formal authority are not the only sources of leadership and that the fluid and complex nature of school improvement requires solidarity among organizational members with collaborative, integrative roles and shared commitment to the school goals. The issue of how to do this in the context of ever-increasing pressures and internal and external conflict is constantly on the minds of principals. And, rhetoric aside, the best way of tracking the distribution of responsibilities is to look at how leadership teams are constructed—who is on them, and how the labor is divided.[14]

Chrispeels and Martin's study of leadership teams in four California schools suggests a number of rules for those who are stepping into expanded leadership roles.[15] We reframe their findings to the context of student support staff to make these suggestions.

- **Think of Your Task Force as a Leadership Team.** Even if it is not wise to give a leadership label to the group, they need to be reminded on a regular basis that they are providing leadership. If the group gels, you can reconfigure it later into your emerging design for cross-role leadership.
- **Charge the Task Force Members With Significant Responsibilities for Communicating.** Chrispeels and Martin note that most teams are willing to accept leadership for communication, but that poor communication structures (e.g., excessive centralization through the administrative structure or infrequent opportunities) often thwart the best intentions of both principals and team members. It is your job to ensure free and frequent communication.
- **Charge the Committee With a Professional Development Role.** As part of their review of different ways of organizing for student support, the team will likely attend workshops and read articles that will not only stimulate learning, but also provide insights and information that should be shared with the rest of the school. Nothing demonstrates leadership more than taking on the task of guiding others through a chance to grow and understand. This kind of reporting is far more interesting to others than just regurgitating information about meetings that occurred or activities that were undertaken.
- **Make Sure That Team Members See Themselves as Part of the Problem-Finding/Problem-Coping Work of the School.** While we have emphasized that finding and solving problems is your role, you can't do it all. A gradual hand-off of problem finding and problem coping to a teacher–student support task force will not, alas, relieve you of all responsibilities, but it does allow you to concentrate your energy on areas in which only you can perform effectively.
- **Allow the Committee to Make Real Decisions.** As the team becomes more expert, you need to give away responsibility for some decisions. Giving away means not second-guessing or evaluating

all decisions. You need to be kept in the loop through regular communication, and reallocation of resources will still need your
approval, but the team will need to feel empowered to really own
the reform process. In an era of accountability and pressure on
principals, this may be your hardest task. In many districts, superintendents are demanding more authoritative, centralized leadership behavior from principals. If you are expected to "control and
command," giving responsibilities away will require some political
astuteness on your part.

CONCLUSION

In Chapter 1, we acknowledged that this book might seem less than compelling to the principal of a school that is under the accountability gun. The
10% solution will not solve all of your problems, nor will it ensure that all
of your students are performing up to their capacity. But we also argued
that thinking outside the box—a box that views student achievement as
the work of teachers and views student support staff as tangential—can
unleash underutilized resources.

The foci of the NASSP report, *Breaking Ranks II*, are all addressed by
reorganizing your student support system:[16]

- **Changing the School's Culture Through Collaborative
  Leadership, Professional Learning Communities, and the
  Strategic Use of Data.** We have focused throughout this book on
  the importance of creating new leadership, enlarging professional
  communities to include the perspectives of student support personnel, and making the student support staff—guardians of student
  data—more involved in data-based decision making.
- **Personalizing the School Environment.** Counselors, social
  workers, and others cannot bear the whole burden of personalizing
  secondary schools, but they have, by training and tradition, been
  among the professionals in schools who have put individualizing
  student services at the center of their work. They have much to
  contribute to this aspect of the long-range reform agenda and
  should be part of the solution.
- **Increasing the Rigor and Quality of Curriculum, Instruction,
  and Assessment.** Student support personnel can, as we have
  demonstrated in several of the cases described in Chapter 4, be
  partners with teachers in improving instruction and assessment.
  In particular, they may be key to helping teachers remove the barriers to learning that make instruction and assessment of student
  achievement difficult. Again, the focus is on support for students
  and teachers.

We have argued that you need to become a change master: Principals are the only people in the school in a position to demand the kind of fundamental change that is being asked here—and the only people who have an understanding of the many moving parts that need to be attended to along the way. Principals need to remove barriers; attend to the preconditions of clarity and relevance, action images, will, and skill; and provide an environment in which hard changes appear rewarding. Whether as a champion or an orchestrator, your skill will be necessary to begin to build the web of change and to sustain it as it grows.

The change process that we have described—starting at the periphery and moving toward the center—is unfashionable with today's "quick fix" reengineering mentality. You have heard about whole-school reform and recommendations such as breaking large high schools into smaller learning communities. We are not necessarily against these models for change, but we do note that they are difficult to implement. Even if your staff (or your district) chooses a whole-school reform initiative, you will still need to deal with the problem of how best to integrate student support into the academic picture. Starting small requires persistence: Looking back at the performance dip model discussed in Chapter 1, we want to reiterate that changes that begin at the margins are often doomed unless there is continued pressure and support over the long haul.

We believe that the destination is worth the effort. Your school will be healthier if all professionals are on the same page, working toward the same goals, and collaborating with their diverse skills and perspectives. You will have a cadre of leaders that includes both teachers and student support personnel, a team that is proactive in problem recognition and in crafting solutions. Your students will have multiple resources to meet their more predictable needs as well as those unexpected life disruptions that keep them from learning. The school, while still a sea of wicked problems, will have additional resources to meet the next wave of demands. The only way to approach a problem of this magnitude is through teamwork—however conceived—to minimize duplication of effort in some areas, wasted effort in others, while ensuring that critical interventions are not missed. Our book is a plea to put the student support professionals you already have in place on that team.

RESOURCES

Sample Job Description 1: Role and Job Description for Student Support Professionals Working in High Schools[17]

School counselors (school guidance counselors and school adjustment counselors) work together and with parents, teachers, and school personnel to support the academic, career, and personal/social development of all students and to ensure that students who are experiencing problems that interfere with learning receive needed support and services through proper referral and follow-up. School counselors support a comprehensive developmental program for all students PreK–12. School counselors collaborate with teachers and other school personnel and support and encourage parental involvement and family partnerships.

School counselors are leaders who advocate for students to ensure equality in access to high-quality learning environments and academic supports. School counselors are highly trained, state-certified professionals who (a) pursue professional growth, (b) display a positive professional attitude, (c) follow the ethical standards outlined by their discipline, (d) attend state and local professional development programs with the support of the school district, (e) join professional associations, (f) read professional journals, and (g) attend relevant workshops and conferences with the support of the school district.

School counselors work towards the goal of spending 80% of their time in school counseling program activities with direct demonstrable benefits to students, and 20% of their time on program management, accountability, evaluation, and professional development activities that support and enhance the program.

Primary Functions

A high school counselor is to provide a comprehensive, developmental program for all students Grades 9–12. The counselor structures activities to meet the needs of students; collaborates with teachers, staff, and parents to enhance their effectiveness in helping students; and works in harmony with school staff to promote the total high school program and student achievement.

Major Job Responsibilities

1. Implement school counseling curriculum to address the Student Development Program and Student Learning Objectives, Grades 9–12.

2. Work with teachers and parents to meet the needs of students through the development of academic, personal, social, and career awareness activities.

3. Counsel small groups and individual students.

4. Consult with teacher, staff, and parents regarding meeting the developmental needs of the students.

5. Refer students with critical needs, in consultation with their parents, to appropriate community resources and follow up on student progress.

6. Participate in counseling activities that contribute to the effective operation of the school.

7. Advocate for all students.

8. Plan, implement, evaluate, and revise the school counseling program.

9. Demonstrate professional conduct and pursue professional growth.

Key Duties

1. Implement the school counseling curriculum: Conduct developmentally sequenced counseling activities in the classroom connected to the Student Development Program and Student Learning Objectives, Grades 9–12, in cooperation with school administrators and teachers. Facilitate the infusion of counseling activities into the regular education curricula to support the developmental needs of students. These activities may include a variety of resources and materials.

2. Work with the teachers and parents to meet the needs of individual students through personal, social, academic, and career awareness activities: Assist administration in orientation activities for new students; facilitate orientation programs for parents and students; and assist students in transition from high school to their next steps connecting to training and education programs. Inform students and their parents of test results and their implications for educational planning and provide resources and information to assist in career awareness, career exploration, and career planning activities.

3. Provide limited counseling for small groups and individual students: Conduct structured, goal-oriented counseling sessions to meet the identified needs of individuals or groups of students. Session topics at the high school level may include self-concept, academic issues, attendance and behavior patterns, conflict resolution, family issues, child abuse, substance abuse prevention, and suicide prevention and intervention as needed. (Students with serious or ongoing psychological counseling needs should be referred to agencies collaborating with the school; see item 6 below.)

4. Advocate for all students: Maintain a current knowledge of equity and diversity issues through district-sponsored professional development; promote equal educational opportunities for all students; provide information to school staff on particular policies relating to all students; assist school staff members in the placement of students with special needs in appropriate programs, such as special education and gifted programs; and promote personalized education for all students where feasible.

5. Consult with teachers, staff, and parents regarding meeting developmental needs of students: Participate in group consultations with school administrators, teachers, parents, and others to enhance their work with students; conduct and facilitate conferences with teachers, students, and parents; and conduct or provide opportunities for parent education programs; and assist families with school-related problems.

6. Refer students with critical needs, in consultation with their parents, to appropriate community resources: Consult and coordinate with in-district professionals and community agencies, such as school psychologists, nurses, administrators, community-based counselors, service agencies, and physicians. Use an effective referral process for assisting students and others to use special programs and services.

7. Participate in activities that contribute to the effective school counseling program within the school: Establish effective liaisons with the various grade levels or instructional departments; act as an advocate for students as appropriate in conjunction with other staff; and assist other school staff in the placement of students with special needs in appropriate programs such as gifted education and special education.

8. Plan, implement, evaluate, and revise the school counseling program: Review the school counseling program at least annually with the district counseling department. Using the appropriate program evaluation tools, review and modify the program components and the program calendar.

9. Demonstrate professional conduct and pursue professional growth: Display a positive professional attitude and follow the ethical standards outlined by the discipline. Attend state and local professional development programs as sponsored by the school district; join professional associations; read professional journals; attend relevant workshops and conferences sponsored by the school district.

Sample Job Description 2: Reporting Relationships[18]

Receives administrative direction from the principal or principal's designee; receives functional and/or technical direction from the assistant principal, secondary counseling services, or other administrative/supervisory staff members designated by the principal.

Functions

Essential Functions:

- Serves at least three assigned periods per day as a member of the counseling, guidance, and student assessment service; cooperates with the school administration and staff in developing student attitudes and behavior that are necessary to maintain proper control, acceptable standards of self-discipline, and a suitable learning environment within the school.
- Counsels individuals and groups of students in the areas of educational, personal, physical, social, and career needs; provides guidance to students in matters regarding graduation, college entrance requirements, and scholarships; consults with parents and school personnel as a means of helping students with educational and personal problems that may be interfering with their learning and success in school.
- Assists in organizing the administration and interpretation of standardized tests; interprets the results of standardized group tests of achievement and scholastic capacity to administrator, parents, and teachers.
- Helps students effectively utilize the educational opportunities of the schools; recommends available resources within the school, school system, and community to meet the needs of individual students; assists in making such referrals and contacts.
- Consults with administration and staff on student referral for supplementary counseling, psychological evaluation, and case conferences.
- Assists in coordinating the gathering of important student records and cooperates with other pupil services staff in scheduled student case conferences; participates in Student Study Team and other problem-solving conferences.
- Serves as a resource person to school personnel and parents regarding the counseling and guidance program.
- Assists in preparation of information for entry on student cumulative records; contributes data concerning student needs to assist in the development of the total educational plan of the school.

- May teach up to two periods per day in the area of guidance or other subjects in accordance with adopted courses of study, if appropriately credentialed.
- Evaluates the performance of subordinate personnel.

Other Functions:

- During periods of critical personnel shortage or other emergency situation, shall temporarily perform any duties, as directed, within the authorization of any credentials held by the incumbent that are registered with the Office of the Los Angeles County Superintendent of Schools and that are a part of the class description requirements in effect at the time such duties are performed.
- Performs other duties as assigned.

Qualifications

Education and Experience Required:

- A bachelor's degree from an accredited college or university.

Desirable Education and Experience:

- Completion of a district-approved internship-type program designed to provide school counseling/guidance experiences while serving as a counseling-assistant.
- Full-time service in a public or private institution while holding a valid teaching credential.
- Experience working with community representatives, diverse ethnic and cultural groups, youth groups, or in social services.
- Experience in individual or group counseling of school-age children.

Knowledge, Skills, Abilities, and Personal Characteristics:

- Knowledge of and experience in the use of counseling and guidance techniques with secondary students.
- Ability to work effectively and cooperatively with colleagues, other district personnel, and community representatives and agencies.
- Knowledge of the growth and development of children and adolescents, learning theory, and mental health concepts.
- Knowledge of the uses and limitations of standardized individual and group tests.
- Ability to communicate effectively with students, parents, and district personnel.
- Ability to work effectively with students in an advisory capacity and with adults in a consultative role.
- Understanding of the relationship between the total educational program and counseling/guidance services.
- Understanding of the physical, intellectual, social, and emotional growth patterns of students.
- Ability to work effectively with all racial, ethnic, linguistic, disability, and socio-economic groups.
- Ability to compose and comprehend written communication.
- Ability to travel to other sites or locations.
- Mobility to traverse all areas of the worksite.

Sample Student Needs Assessment Questionnaire[19]

1. **I have met with a counselor individually at <u>this</u> school about . . .** (Fill in all that apply)
   __Academic progress   __Career information   __College information
   __Testing   __Scheduling issues   __Discipline
   __Attendance   __Other school problems   __Personal/Family issues
   __Course selection   __I have not spoken with a counselor

2. **I have seen a counselor in a group setting (e.g., classroom, advisory, support group) at this school about . . .** (Fill in all that apply)
   __Academic progress   __Career information   __College information
   __Testing   __Scheduling issues   __Discipline
   __Attendance   __Other school problems   __Personal/Family issues
   __Course selection   __I have not spoken with a counselor

3. **I have met with a social worker individually at <u>this</u> school about . . .** (Fill in all that apply)
   __Study skills   __Career information   __Personal/Family issues
   __Testing   __Discipline   __Attendance
   __Other school problems __I have not spoken with a social worker

4. **I have met with a social worker in a group setting (e.g., classroom, advisory, support group) at this school about . . .** (Fill in all that apply)
   __Study skills   __Career information   __Personal/Family issues
   __Testing   __Discipline   __Attendance
   __Other school problems __I have not spoken with a social worker

5. **Please indicate if you have met individually or in a group setting with any other student support professional:**
   __School psychologist
   __Chemical dependency specialist
   __School nurse
   __Home-community liaison
   __Study skills

6. **How many times have you met with/seen a student support person this school year?** (Fill in one)
   __Zero   __One or two   __Three or four   __Five or six   __Seven or more

7. **If you have gone to a student support person with a concern, has he or she been helpful?** (Fill in one)
   __Yes   __No   __Sometimes

8. **Was your counselor available when you needed to see her/him?** (Fill in one)
   __Yes   __No   __Sometimes   __I have not needed to see a counselor

9. **Was your social worker available when you needed to see her/him?** (Fill in one)
   __Yes   __No   __Sometimes   __I have not needed to see a social worker

10. **I would like to talk to someone about the following:** (Fill in all that apply)
    __Learning how to recognize   __How to choose and make friends
    my interests and abilities   __Creating a plan for high school and beyond
    __Learning how to better   __Learning about post–high school choices
    communicate with others   __How to get involved in school activities
    __A personal problem   __Drug and alcohol issues
    __How to use my time wisely   __Family/Living arrangements
    __Discussing personal and school safety
    __Other areas:
    (Please specify what they are below)

    _____
    _____
    _____

11. I feel safe in my school.

    ◯   ◯   ◯   ◯

Strongly Agree   Agree   Disagree   Strongly Disagree

12. My teachers believe that all students can do well.

    ◯   ◯   ◯   ◯

Strongly Agree   Agree   Disagree   Strongly Disagree

13. I feel that I am a part of this school.

    ◯   ◯   ◯   ◯

Strongly Agree   Agree   Disagree   Strongly Disagree

14. My teachers set high expectations for all students.

    ◯   ◯   ◯   ◯

Strongly Agree   Agree   Disagree   Strongly Disagree

15. The adults in my school care about students.

    ◯   ◯   ◯   ◯

Strongly Agree   Agree   Disagree   Strongly Disagree

16. I am satisfied with the quality of the education I receive at my school.

    ◯   ◯   ◯   ◯

Strongly Agree   Agree   Disagree   Strongly Disagree

17. There is at least one adult in my school I can talk to who knows me well.

    ◯   ◯   ◯   ◯

Strongly Agree   Agree   Disagree   Strongly Disagree

18. Students in my school show respect for students who work hard and do well.

    ◯   ◯   ◯   ◯

Strongly Agree   Agree   Disagree   Strongly Disagree

19. I am taking classes that challenge me.

    ◯   ◯   ◯   ◯

Strongly Agree   Agree   Disagree   Strongly Disagree

20. Graduating from high school is important to me.

    ◯   ◯   ◯   ◯

Strongly Agree   Agree   Disagree   Strongly Disagree

21. I know what I need to do to graduate from my high school.

    ◯   ◯   ◯   ◯

Strongly Agree   Agree   Disagree   Strongly Disagree

22. I believe it is important to attend school <u>every day</u>.

○	○	○	○
Strongly Agree	Agree	Disagree	Strongly Disagree

23. How much time do you spend in school <u>talking about</u> your future? (Fill in one)

○	○	○
Often	Sometimes	Never

24. At my school, I am a member of . . . (Fill in all that apply)

__A small learning community   __An "academy"
__A "house"   __I don't know

25. I am in an "advisory" or "foundations" group in my school. (Fill in one)

__Yes   __No   __I don't know

26. If you are part of an advisory/foundations group, what things do you usually do during advisory time? (Fill in all that apply)

__Explore my interests and abilities   __Develop decision-making and problem-solving
__Learn how to communicate with others   skills
__Discuss personal problems   __Create a plan for high school and beyond
__Learn how to use my time wisely   __Learn about post–high school choices
__Discuss personal and school safety   __Discuss how to get involved in school activities
__Attendance is taken   __Discuss how to choose and make friends
__Talk to my friends   __Do homework
__Read   __Sleep/take naps
__I do not attend advisory/foundations   __Review my academic progress
  group on a regular basis
__Other areas (Please specify)

_____

_____

27. Who do you go to when you have a problem or concern? (Select no more than five from the list below)

__Parent   __Friend   __Counselor
__School social worker   __Teacher/Coach   __School nurse
__Relative (not parent)   __School administrator   __Pastor/Rabbi/Minister/
__Someone else   __I would not go to   Other religious leader
                            anyone if I had a problem

Thanks. Our goal is to offer better services to students.

Appendix

Research Methods

Our research included several distinct data collection activities that took place between 1999 and 2004. We describe them briefly below. For more information about data collection and analysis, please contact the first author, Karen Seashore Louis.

Our investigation of the role of student development personnel was initially funded by the Wallace Foundation as part of the larger study of the Transforming School Counseling Initiative (TSCI). More information about the larger study is available at http://education.umn.edu/CAREI/Reports/docs/TSCI_Final.pdf. As part of the study, one-week site visits were conducted in late fall and winter of 1999–2000, and again in the subsequent three years to six districts that were collaborating in the study. The districts (which were not promised confidentiality) were

- Los Angeles Unified School District, California
- Vigo County Public School Corporation, Indiana
- Columbus Public Schools, Ohio
- Athens-Clarke County Public Schools, Georgia
- Clayton County Public Schools, Georgia
- Duval County Public Schools, Florida

During the first two years, two- or three-member teams interviewed counselor supervisors at the district level as well as practicing counselors and principals in at least one elementary, middle, and high school across the site. In the last two years, one person conducted more limited interviews with counselors-in-training and practicing counselors. We also gathered documents that would further inform the evaluation. Interviews were subsequently transcribed, yielding approximately 200 single-spaced pages of case studies based on all materials available for each site.

As part of the Wallace Foundation study, we also conducted a survey of practicing counselors. These data were collected in collaboration with the school counseling faculty of the six universities that were funded by the

Wallace Foundation to engage in preparing counselors to do "transformed" work. Each of the universities administered the survey during a countywide or statewide professional meeting to all practicing counselors attending that meeting. The completed surveys were sent to us for analysis.

In 2003, again funded by the Wallace Foundation, we extended our emerging interest in the role of principals. In this mini-study, we interviewed 15 principals and a district administrator in four districts in Florida and Minnesota who had not previously been part of our sample. Seven of the principals were in middle schools, and 7 were in high schools. One of the principals had been a high school principal for 15 years and is now an elementary school principal. We selected Minnesota and Florida as sites because neither state has mandatory legislative language relating to school counselors; additionally, the districts in this new sample all operate under site-based management. Although Florida is a TSCI state, not all of the schools participated or received funding to be a part of the initiative. We chose Minnesota both because it was *not* part of the TSCI study and because some areas of the state have school counseling reform initiatives being tested in a number of high schools beginning this year. The questions we asked the principals were designed to give a comprehensive analysis of whether or not the principals had a vision or a coherent standard for their nonteaching student service professionals. In addition, the questions helped assess the ways in which principals choose to deploy their nonteaching staff during times of fiscal and accountability pressure.

We were fortunate to expand our data collection from counselors to a district closer to home starting in 2003. Our data from the Saint Paul Public Schools were collected as part of the initiative titled Connected Counseling, funded by the Bush Foundation. Our data includes lead counselor and counseling team interviews, student surveys, steering committee meeting notes, and interviews with the Connected Counseling coordinator. Again, most of our information comes from interviews with school and district administrators and school counselors involved in the effort to reform school counseling within the Saint Paul schools.

Data analysis was based, except for the brief survey analysis presented in Chapter 3, on detailed analysis of interview transcripts. We did not use a qualitative software program, but hand-coded items that related to the role of the counselors, teachers, principals, and district administrators. The limited survey analysis that we present was conducted using SPSS (Statistical Package for the Social Sciences) software.

Endnotes

CHAPTER 1

1. NASSP, 2004.
2. Another term widely used to refer to nonteaching professional staff in schools is *student development*.
3. Bracy, 2003.
4. Barton, 2005; Brown, 1999; National Center for Education Statistics, 2001.
5. Information on the Third International Math and Science Study can be found at www.timss.org. High between-school variation in student learning is an indicator of inequality, because it suggests that some students are being given greater opportunities to learn than others.
6. NASSP, 2004.
7. Borman, Hewes, Overman, & Brown, 2002; Traub, 1999.
8. Berends, Kirby, Naftel, & McKelvey, 2001.
9. Porter, Kirst, Osthoff, Smithson, & Schneider, 1993.
10. Elmore & Fuhrman, 1994.
11. DiPaola & Tschannen-Moran, 2003.
12. DiPaola & Tschannen-Moran, 2003, p. 43.
13. Education Trust, 2003.
14. Leithwood, Louis, Anderson, & Wahlstrom, 2004.
15. DiPaola & Tschannen-Moran, 2003.
16. Odden & Archibald, 2000.
17. Schmoker, 1999.
18. Parsad, Alexander, Ferris, Hudson, & Greene, 2003.
19. Picus, 2001.
20. Tirozzi & Ferrandino, 2003.
21. Kanter, 1983.
22. Mason & Mitroff, 1981.
23. Bryk, Easton, Kerbow, Rollow, & Sebring, 1993.
24. Sarason, 1971.
25. Adapted from Louis & Miles, 1990, Chapter 12.
26. Hall & Hord, 1987.
27. Louis, 1994.
28. Eastwood & Louis, 1992.
29. Huberman & Miles, 1984.
30. Fullan, 1993; Hall & Hord, 1987; Kotter, 1995.

31. Firestone, 1996.
32. Smylie, Conley, & Marks, 2002, p. 171.
33. Gronn, 2000.

CHAPTER 2

1. Herr, 2002.
2. Murphy, Beck, Crawford & Hodges, 2001.
3. Herr, 2002.
4. Dupper & Evans, 1996.
5. See, for example, the Coalition for Community Schools at www.community schools.org.
6. National Commission on Excellence in Education,1983.
7. Herr, 2002.
8. Herr, 2002.
9. Martin, 2002.
10. Allen-Meares, 1994.
11. Lapan, Gysbers, & Sun, 1997.
12. Nelson & Gardner, 1998.
13. Nelson & Gardner, 1998.
14. Brigman & Campbell, 2003.
15. Blum, 2004.
16. Education Trust, n.d.
17. The Education Trust's Web site contains a great deal of material that is useful for school-based practitioners. See www.edtrust.org.
18. The Wallace Foundation's current initiatives and focus are available on their Web site, www.wallacefunds.org.
19. Martin, 2002, p. 148.
20. Martin, 2002, p. 151.
21. Our evaluation of the TSCI initiative also emphasizes its impact on university programs and their graduates. For more information, see the evaluation Web site education .umn.edu/CAREI/Reports/default.html, or contact Karen Seashore Louis.
22. Bemak, Keys, & Lockhart, 1998.
23. ASCA, 2003.
24. Hatch & Bowers, 2003, p. 8.
25. Hatch & Bowers, 2003, p. 49.
26. Hatch & Bowers, 2003, p. 49.
27. Hatch & Bowers, 2003, p. 17.
28. Hatch & Bowers, 2003, pp. 81–86.
29. Hatch & Bowers, 2003. p. 34.
30. Brown, 1999.

CHAPTER 3

1. Meyer, 1983.
2. Fennell, 1999.
3. Hardesty & Miller, 1994.

4. Handy, 1993.
5. Schein, 1992.
6. Chatman & Jehn, 1984; Swidler, 1983.
7. Cohen & March, 1972; Lagerweij, Louis, & Voogt, 1998.
8. We have chosen not to report the statistical procedures used to analyze the survey, but we are happy to provide more methodological information as well as the survey data to anyone who is interested. The number of counselors responding totaled 1012, including 46.3% elementary, 22.9% middle, and 30.7% senior high counselors.
9. Allen-Meares, 1994.
10. Allen-Meares, 1994, p. 560.
11. Allen-Meares, 1994, p. 566.
12. This section draws heavily on Seppanen & Sears, 2002.
13. Hart & Jacobi, 1992.

CHAPTER 4

1. Keys & Lockhart, 1999, p. 101.
2. Keys & Lockhart, 1999, p. 103.
3. Kaplan & Evans, 1999.
4. House & Hayes, 2002.

CHAPTER 5

1. Lewin, 1951.
2. Our description is adapted from a public access Web site for health care professionals (www.qaproject.org/methods/resforcefield.html).
3. Two that we find useful: D. M. Boje's Web page at New Mexico State University (cbae.nmsu.edu/~dboje/sbc/pages/page3.html) and an overview of SWOT by Business balls.com (www.businessballs.com/swotanalysisfreetemplate.htm).
4. This finding is from the survey portion of the study reported in Louis and Miles (1990). It was not, however, included in that book.
5. Elmore, 1987.
6. Brunner, 2002.
7. Hatch, 2002, p. 207.
8. Hatch, 2002.
9. From erc.msh.org/quality/describe.cfm.
10. From erc.msh.org/quality/analyze.cfm.
11. From erc.msh.org/quality/plnsol.cfm.
12. Deming, 1982.
13. From erc.msh.org/quality/impsol.cfm.
14. From erc.msh.org/quality/moneval.cfm.
15. This section provides a short summary of Patricia Hatch's unpublished doctoral research (Hatch, 2002).
16. Hatch, 2002, p. 104.
17. Hatch, 2002, pp. 187, 189, 191, 194.

CHAPTER 6

1. Kotter, 1995.
2. Luecke, 2003, p. 43.
3. Wahlstrom & Louis, 1993.
4. Louis, 1998.
5. MacDuffie, 1997.
6. Turner, 1976.
7. Louis & Miles, 1990.
8. Louis & Miles, 1990, p. 286.
9. Scharmer, 1999.
10. Heifetz, 1994.
11. Firestone, 1996; Pounder, Ogawa, & Adams, 1995.
12. Smylie, Conley, & Marks, 2002, p. 172.
13. Pounder, Ogawa, & Adams, 1995.
14. Gronn, 2000.
15. Chrispeels & Martin, 2002.
16. NASSP, 2004.
17. This job description is adapted from the Springfield (Massachusetts) School District Professional Standards, available at www.umass.edu/schoolcounseling/PDFs/SpringfieldSchoolDistrictProfessionalStandards.pdf. This Web site includes similar material for elementary and middle school counselors.
18. This job description comes from www.teachinla.com/cert/counselor.html.
19. This survey was created by a team of counselors, district administrators, evaluators, and smaller learning community coordinators in the St. Paul Public Schools, Fall 2003. This survey has been slightly modified by the authors of this book to include other student support professionals.

References

Allen-Meares, P. (1994). Social work services in schools: A national study of entry-level tasks. *Social Work, 39*(5), 560–566.

American School Counselor Association. (1997). *The national standards for school counseling programs.* Alexandria, VA: Author.

American School Counselor Association. (2003). The ASCA national model: A framework for school counseling programs. *Professional School Counseling, 6*(3), 165–168.

Barton, P. (2005). *Parsing the achievement gap: Baselines for tracking progress.* Princeton, NJ: Educational Testing Service.

Bemak, F., Keys, S. G., & Lockhart, E. (1998). Transforming school counseling to serve the mental health needs of at-risk youth. *Journal of Counseling and Development, 76*(4), 381–388.

Berends, M., Kirby, S. N., Naftel, S., & McKelvey, C. (2001). *Implementation and performance in new American schools: Three years into scale-up.* Santa Monica, CA: RAND.

Blum, R. (2004). Wingspread declaration on school connections. *Journal of School Health, 74*(7), 233–234.

Borman, G., Hewes, G., Overman, L., & Brown, S. (2002). *Comprehensive school reform and student achievement: A meta-analysis.* Baltimore, MD: Johns Hopkins University Press.

Bracy, G. (2003). April foolishness: The 20th anniversary of a nation at risk. *Phi Delta Kappan, 84*(8), 616–621.

Brigman, G., & Campbell, C. (2003). Helping students improve academic achievement and school success behavior. *Professional School Counseling, 7,* 91–98.

Brown, D. (1999). Improving academic achievement: What school counselors can do. Greensboro: University of North Carolina, ERIC Counseling and Student Services Clearinghouse.

Brunner, C. C. (2002). Professing educational administration: Conceptions of power. *Journal of School Leadership, 12,* 693–720.

Bryk, A. S., Easton, J. Q., Kerbow, D., Rollow, S. G., & Sebring, P. A. (1993). *A view from the elementary schools: The state of reform in Chicago.* Chicago: University of Chicago, The Consortium on Chicago School Research.

Chatman, J., & Jehn, K. (1984). Assessing the relationship between industry characteristics and organizational cultures: How different can you be? *Academy of Management Review, 37*(3), 522–553.

Chrispeels, J. H., & Martin, K. J. (2002). Four school leadership teams define their roles within organizational and political structures to improve student learning. *School Effectiveness and School Improvement, 13*(3), 327–365.

Cohen, M. D., & March, J. G. (1972). A garbage can model of organizational choice. *Administrative Science Quarterly, 17*(1), 1–25.

Deming, W. E. (1982). *Quality, productivity and competitive position.* Cambridge, MA: MIT Press.

DiPaola, M., & Tschannen-Moran, M. (2003). The principalship at a crossroads: A study of the conditions and concerns of principals. *NASSP Bulletin, 87*(634), 43–65.

Dupper, D. R., & Evans, S. (1996). From band-aids and putting out fires to prevention: School social work practice approaches for the new century. *Social Work in Education, 18*(3), 187–192.

Eastwood, K., & Louis, K. S. (1992). Restructuring that lasts: Managing the performance dip. *School Leadership, 2*(2), 212–225.

Education Trust. (n.d.). *School Counseling is . . . .* Retrieved August 30, 2004, from www2 .edtrust.org/edtrust/Transforming+School+Counseling/counseling+background.

Education Trust. (2003). *Improving Achievement and Closing Gaps between Groups* [PowerPoint presentation to the Minnesota Department of Education]. Retrieved August 30, 2004, from www.edtrust.org.

Elmore, R. (1987). Instruments and strategy in public policy. *Policy Studies Review, 7*(2), 174–186.

Elmore, R. F., & Fuhrman, S. (1994). *The governance of the curriculum.* Alexandria, VA: Association for Supervision and Curriculum Development.

Fennell, H. A. (1999). Feminine faces of leadership: Beyond structural-functionalism? *Journal of School Leadership, 9*(3), 254–285.

Firestone, W. (1996). Leadership role or functions? In K. Leithwood, J. Champman, D. Corson, P. Hallinger, & A. Hart (Eds.), *International handbook of educational leadership and administration* (pp. 395–418). Dordrecht, The Netherlands: Kluwer.

Fullan, M. (1993). *Change forces: Probing the depths of educational reform.* New York: Falmer.

Gronn, P. (2000). Distributed properties: A new architecture for leadership. *Educational Management & Administration, 28*(3), 317–338.

Hall, G., & Hord, S. (1987). *Change in schools: Facilitating the process.* Albany, NY: SUNY Press.

Handy, C. (1993). *Understanding organizations.* Oxford, England: Oxford University Press.

Hardesty, P., & Miller, J. (1994). The role of elementary school counselors compared with their middle and secondary school counterparts. *Elementary School Guidance & Counseling, 29*(2), 83–91.

Hart, P., & Jacobi, J. (1992). *From gatekeeper to advocate: Transforming the role of the school counselor.* New York: College Entrance Board.

Hatch, P. A. (2002). *National standards for school counseling programs: A source of legitimacy or of reform?* Unpublished doctoral dissertation, University of California at Riverside.

Hatch, P. A., & Bowers, J. (2003). *The ASCA National Model: A Framework for School Counseling Programs.* Alexandria, VA: The American School Counselor Association.

Heifetz, R. (1994). *Leadership without easy answers.* Boston, MA: Belknap.

Herr, E. L. (2002). School reform and perspectives on the role of school counselors: A century of proposals for change. *Professional School Counseling, 5*(4), 236–245.

House, R. M., & Hayes, R. L. (2002). School counselors: Becoming key players in school reform. *Professional School Counseling, 5*(4), 249–256.

Huberman, A. M., & Miles, M. B. (1984). *Innovation up close: How school improvement works.* New York: Plenum.

Kanter, R. M. (1983). *The change masters: Innovation for productivity in the American corporation.* New York: Simon & Schuster.

Kaplan, L. S., & Evans, M. W. (1999). Hiring the best counseling candidates to promote students' achievement. *NASSP Bulletin, 83*(603), 34–39.

Keys, S. G., & Lockhart, E. (1999). The school counselor's role in facilitating multisystemic change. *Professional School Counseling, 3*(2), 101–107.

Kotter, J. P. (1995). Leading change: Why transformation efforts fail. *Harvard Business Review on Change, 73*(2), 59.

Lagerweij, N., Louis, K. S., & Voogt, J. (1998). School development and organizational learning: Toward an integrative theory. In K. Leithwood & K. S. Louis (Eds.), *Organizational learning in schools* (pp. 237–260). Lisse, The Netherlands: Swets and Zeitlinger.

Lapan, R. T., Gysbers, N. C., & Sun, Y. (1997). The impact of more fully implemented guidance programs on the school experiences of high school students: A statewide evaluation study. *Journal of Counseling & Development, 75,* 292–302.

Leithwood, K., Louis, K. S., Anderson, S., & Wahlstrom, K. (2004). *How leadership influences student learning: A review of research.* Retrieved July 31, 2005, from www.wallace foundation.org/WF/KnowledgeCenter/KnowledgeTopics/EducationLeadership/How LeadershipInfluencesStudentLearning.htm.

Lewin, K. (1951). *Field theory in social science: Selected theoretical papers.* New York: Harper.

Louis, K. S. (1994). Beyond "managed change": Rethinking how schools improve. *School Effectiveness and School Improvement, 5*(1), 1–22.

Louis, K. S. (1998). Effects of teacher quality of work life in secondary schools on commitment and sense of efficacy. *School Effectiveness and School Improvement, 9*(1), 1–27.

Louis, K. S., & Miles, M. B. (1990). *Improving the urban high school: What works and why.* New York: Teachers College Press.

Luecke, R. (2003). Managing change and transition. *Harvard Business Essentials* Boston: Harvard Business School Press.

MacDuffie, J. P. (1997). The road to "root cause": Shop-floor problem-solving at three auto assembly plants. *Management Science, 43*(4), 479–502.

Martin, P. (2002). Transforming school counseling: A national perspective. *Theory Into Practice, 41*(3), 148–153.

Mason, R. O, & Mitroff, I. (1981). *Challenging strategic planning assumptions: Theory, cases, and techniques.* New York: Wiley.

Meyer, J. (1983). Institutionalization and the rationality of organizational structure. In J. Meyer & W. R. Scott (Eds.), *Organizational environment: Ritual and rationality* (pp. 261–282). Beverly Hills, CA: Sage.

Murphy, J., Beck, L. G., Crawford, M., & Hodges, A. (2001). *The productive high school: Creating personalized academic communities.* Thousand Oaks, CA: Corwin.

National Association of Secondary School Principals. (2004). *Breaking ranks II: Strategies for leading high school reform.* Reston, VA: Author.

National Center for Education Statistics. (2001). *Educational achievement and black-white inequality.* Washington, DC: U.S. Department of Education.

National Commission on Excellence in Education. (1983). *A nation at risk: The imperative for educational reform.* Washington, DC: U.S. Department of Education.

Nelson, D. E., & Gardner, J. L. (1998). *An evaluation of the comprehensive program in Utah public schools.* Salt Lake City, UT: Utah State Office of Education.

Odden, A., & Archibald, S. (2000). Reallocating resources to support higher student achievement: An empirical look at five sites. *Journal of Educational Finance, 25*(4), 545–564.

Parsad, B., Alexander, D., Ferris, E., Hudson, L., & Greene, B. (2003). High school guidance counseling. *E.D. Tabs,* 124 [Occasional Paper]. Washington, DC: National Center for Educational Statistics.

Picus, L. O. (2001). *In search of more productive schools: A guide to resource allocation.* Eugene, OR: University of Oregon, ERIC Clearinghouse on Educational Management.

Porter, A. C., Kirst, M. W., Osthoff, E. J., Smithson, J. S., & Schneider, S. A. (1993). *Reform up close: An analysis of high school mathematics and science classrooms* (Final report to the National Science Foundation on Grant No. SPA-8953446 to the Consortium for Policy Research in Education). Madison: University of Wisconsin at Madison, Wisconsin Center for Education Research.

Pounder, D. G, Ogawa, R. T., & Adams, E. A. (1995). Leadership as an organizational phenomenon: Its impact on school performance. *Educational Administration Quarterly, 31*(4), 564–588.

Sarason, S. B. (1971). *The culture of the school and the problem of change.* Boston: Allyn & Bacon.

Scharmer, R. O. (1999). *Adaptive change: What's essential and what's expendable? A conversation with Ron Heifetz.* Retrieved August 19, 2004, from www.dialogonleadership.org/Heifetz-1999.html#seven.

Schein, E. (1992). *Organizational culture and leadership* (2nd ed.). San Francisco: Jossey Bass.

Schmoker, M. (1999). *Results: The key to continuous school improvement.* Arlington, VA: Association for Supervision and Curriculum Development.

Seppanen, P., & Sears, S. (2002, November). *Advocates and backbenchers.* Paper presented at the University Council for Educational Administration, Portland, OR.

Smylie, M. A., Conley, S. S., & Marks, H. M. (2002). Exploring new approaches to teacher leadership for school improvement. In J. Murphy (Ed.), *The educational leadership challenge: Redefining leadership for the 21st century* (pp. 162–188). Chicago: University of Chicago Press.

Swidler, A. (1983). Culture in action: Symbols and strategies. *American Sociological Review, 51*(2), 273–286.

Tirozzi, G. N., & Ferrandino, V. L. (2003, March 5). The sad state of states. *Education Week.*

Traub, J. (1999). *Better by design.* Washington, DC: Thomas B. Fordham Foundation. Retrieved August 11, 2004, from www.edexcellence.net/library/bbd/better_by_design.

Turner, B. A. (1976). The organizational and interorganizational development of disasters. *Administrative Science Quarterly, 21*(3), 378–397.

Wahlstrom, K., & Louis, K. S. (1993). Adoption revisited: Decision-making and school district policy. In S. Bachrach & R. Ogawa (Eds.), *Advances in research and theories of school management and educational policy* (pp. 61–119). Greenwich, CT: JAI.

Index

CORWIN PRESS

The Corwin Press logo—a raven striding across an open book—represents the union of courage and learning. Corwin Press is committed to improving education for all learners by publishing books and other professional development resources for those serving the field of PreK–12 education. By providing practical, hands-on materials, Corwin Press continues to carry out the promise of its motto: **"Helping Educators Do Their Work Better."**